The Lucky Lotus

The filthy dirty life of an adopted East Indian girl in an alabaster world

PUSHPA DEVI

The Lucky Lotus

Copyright © 2022 by Pushpa Devi

ISBN: 979-8-9876679-4-1

Book Designer: Sarah Katreen Hoggatt

10 9 8 7 6 5 4 3 2 1

This book also available in digital formats.

CONTENTS

SWEET LILAC ❀ 1

SACRED TREE ❀ 10

POINSETTIA DOLL ❀ 20

PERFUMED DAISY ❀ 29

GLADIOLUS ❀ 41

DAFFODIL ❀ 46

COW PARSLEY ❀ 54

CHRYSANTHEMUM CITIZEN ❀ 64

CHAMPA LEI ❀ 75

CAMELLIA GINGER ❀ 90

PLUM BLOSSOMS ❀ 98

PLUCKED FLOWER BLOSSOMS ❀ 114

MUSTANG LOTUS ❀ 130

ABOUT THE AUTHOR ❀ 145

Sweet Lilac
मीठा बकाइन

S OME SOUTHERN ACCENTS ARE LIKE NAILS *on a chalkboard especially if they are peppered with unwanted truth.*

"Root to rise and remember your breath is all y'all have. Split yourself wide open."

It is early spring in Florida and all we care about is not looking like a beached whale but Kelly, with her blonde high-perched ponytail and screechy twang, persists in forcing us to look at yoga as more than sculpting our body.

"To grow we must get uncomfortable, and to blossom, it takes unraveling of that shit we use to define ourselves."

How in the hell did I even get to this point of following an Alabama country girl to a place of feeling my emotions day after day?

Moving intentionally through each pose during this hot yoga class is melting off physical and mental toxins. It is awful but for some stupid reason, I keep coming back to contort my body in a room that is over 100 degrees with a person whose voice annoys me. Noticing that I am the token East Indian person in the room of entitled white people twisting in coordinating Lululemon outfits brings on insecurities. They are entitled because they can pay for the Lululemon clothing. I protest and still wear Target.

Nothing new. It is always that way. Me the odd one in every room.

"Take a deep breath in and make it sound like a powerful large wave roaring. Exhale and empty like the ocean sound when it recedes to a lull."

She is irritating but has such command of the room that we all give in to her every whim.

"Find your way to Warrior II. Bring your hands down through your heart center and reach one arm to the back wall and the other to the front of the room. Reach as far as you can while keeping that lunge as low as you can go."

The guy next to me keeps gasping for air and fidgeting. He comes out of Warrior II and drops to the floor in child's pose: a resting pose on hands and knees with forehead on the floor. My thighs are on fire. I try to hold perfection on my mat while my ego wants to beat the guy next to me. I am determined to not end up on the mat like him.

"Y'all are too comfortable in your comfort zone. You can only grow if you smile and play by trying on something new."

I fake a smile but want to yell.

What the hell? I'm already out of my comfort zone?!

The robotic class obeys Kelly's demands to push and transcend the movements even as some people are falling out. My determined mind gets me to that place of pain and clinging to my breath, I time travel beyond the pose to a place deep into my heart. The treasure chest shrouding my iconic Daddy hides away here.

"Snip here Daddy?" The menthol aroma of Aqua Velva gel hovers like a halo in his thick, combed, jet-black hair. "I'm a good hair cutter, right, Daddy?"

This pretending game, which we do most nights, is fun. My tiny body struggles to reach over the back of his black leather recliner. It pushes under my armpits while reaching from behind to style his hair. He starts to fall asleep.

Mama D comes barreling around the corner.

"Why are you not helping me with dinner, Pushpa?"

"There you go Daddy. Oh, let me just fix this one part here. I want to do a good job. I think you will like it so much!" Ignoring her is my response since that is what Daddy does.

"BREATHE IN AND SINK EVEN lower." Kelly's toe flicks the end of my mat as she creeps around the room causing my eyes to flutter open for a second.

"Know that you are capable of dredging deeper. Y'all want to reach for greatness but are not willing to unload your stuff here on the mat."

What the hell does she want from me? I would love to unload on her right now!

"What you do on this mat is exactly what you do in the world out there. Hold back."

Can I just be comfortable for once and not have to constantly heal and grow? It is old having to deal with so much pain. Everyone else seems to have a much easier life than I do. "It's up to you: leave it on your mat or carry it out there to affect others."

Kelly stands in front of me looking me right in the eye. I close my eyes to escape to a familiar pain. The iconic daddy appears behind my eyelids again. This time a daddy in his seventies with white hair. His sharp brown eyes standing out from this white German face and bulbous nose. His heart wears on his face when he looks at me.

Daddy and I are driving home in his Salsa Red 1987 Nissan Pathfinder on a depressing and gloomy mid-December afternoon.

"That was a fun lunch. Thanks for taking me out." Even in my forties he will not allow me to pay for our lunch.

Why do I always feel like a child still when we are together?

"You're a lead foot, Pooh."

Daddy is legally blind and cannot do one of his favorite things which is driving. It is hard to watch him lose his independence.

"Well, I learned from the best lead foot of them all."

He smirks as we roll to a stop in front of the oversized garage built for his rocks and lapidary equipment. The child-like fear of upsetting my dad forms a lump in my throat, but the anger I feel wants to unleash the bold woman in me. It's not that I am angry with him but with the situation. I slump over the steering wheel and sigh while gathering my thoughts. The rain taps the window and begins to cocoon us in without a view of the outside world.

"Why didn't you stand up for me?!" It came out like an ugly cry and less controlled than I had planned.

Daddy's brown eyes begin to puddle up. I see that he is hurting but I cannot stop. I must make my last plea with him to change Mama D's mind.

"Can you please *do something?!* The land you are giving to Marie is *mine.* Why are you letting Mama D give it to her?!"

My sister is conniving and has somehow made her way onto their sympathetic side.

"Well?" The bitterness seethes through me knowing that I am treated differently. I am always the outsider with the brown skin and no blood relation to them.

"I am so sorry but there is nothing I can do," he says as he breaks down and cries. "I know it is unfair. It has been yours since you were small." It is unnerving to see my dad cry. He is the rock in my life.

Feeling deflated, I take a deep breath and soften a little. "Look, everyone got their land and sold it. The one parcel left had *my* name on it, and I had *no* intention of selling it. It was important to me to keep it in the family, and I have dreamed about building on it for years. Now that dream is gone."

My gaze is steady towards him. He listens but will not look at me. I see a man of deep sorrow carrying heavy regret. His spirit is broken down from years of berating from Mama D. He now looks small as he cries, hunched over, looking down.

"I am sorry. I know you feel bad, but I feel shafted. It is unfair."

The anger bubbles up again and I am shaking inside. *No, I am not sorry. Shattered dreams and wasted time planting stupid plants and trees on my homesite. This just tells me even more that I am the "adopted" one.*

"Apparently, only blood family can inherit a piece of land. It is just unfair, and I wish you would stand up to that woman who is your wife and stop this! You are her husband!"

He continues with his quivering voice while holding back his emotions, "I am sorry Pooh, I know it is unfair to you."

Do you?! Do you really?! Damn it, get a set of balls and fight for me!

The effects of the decades-long marriage to a woman who has dominated his life drapes over his body like a wet wool blanket. He has been powerless, emasculated, and passive to her every whim for forty years.

Why in the hell didn't he leave or say something? Why does he not have any say in the matter? My iconic father loses footing from his golden pedestal and is now just another victim of Mama D.

"I know it is unfair but your mother, Shirley, is going to do what she wants," he mumbles under his deflated ego. Straddling between feeling sorry for my father and sorry for myself, we bond over our victimhood. Once again, Mama D wins.

"BE A WARRIOR IN YOUR life: strong but soft. What y'all do here on the mat is a mirror image of how you are in your life. Be powerful without being hard. Either full on or hanging out are the only choices."

While in a sweaty Warrior II pose, the memory of my dad's pained face fades into the wall I am staring at. No longer will I fight for it but rather surrender to what is and let things happen without trying to control anymore.

"It's not worth fighting for. You know your mother," I remember him saying.

WHEN MAMA D DIES A new man emerges out of Daddy. He calls one night to tell me his news.

"Hi Pooh' He stammers, "I have something to tell you, I think I am in love."

I have prayed so many times for Daddy to feel loved and now unconditional love and kindness has found a way to Daddy after fifty years of hell. Hope is renewed!

"Daddy, you seem so happy with Miss Kitty," I say during an afternoon visit. His eyes light up and I see a man who has been hidden for decades. He comes to life.

"Your dad is just wonderful and he is so handsome." Miss Kitty grabs his cheek and looks at him with adoration. Seeing Daddy loved is so strange. Mama D never showed affection for Daddy, only disdain.

Unfortunately, Miss Kitty began to show signs of dementia and her family took her away to a place that could help her. As the disease took over, she became mean, and Daddy's little lady slipped from his arms.

"Daddy, I am so sorry for what has happened. It was so good to see you loved and respected and it brings me joy to see that you finally got to be loved in the way you deserve."

Real love does happen if you are patient and kind. I need to believe that!

He took a deep breath and sighed, "It is just good that we had the time we did."

His life was empty again with only a room to live in and no dog as a companion. His eyes changed to a lighter shade and started to sparkle in an unusual way.

My gut pulls me back to him on a late July day. He is not sick, he is not dying, but something in me knows this is it. I know this is the last time to see him.

This man, the scientist who had accomplished great things like determining the melting point of hafnium, the man who earned a high school diploma in three years, the man who earned a bachelor's degree in physics in three years, greets me with his hat on. I see he has begun to decline.

He is smaller and has shrunk like old people do, but still carries a big heart that gets excited to see me as much as I do to see him. He lives in a house with several others who also require a place to live with constant supervision. This would be his home for his last year of life.

Handsome as ever with his air of dignity, he still wears the button-up shirt with the pocket to carry his black pen that still says, "U.S. Government." This big man in a little old man's body has been three thousand miles away for the last twenty-five years. Oh, how I missed him.

"Pooh, is that you?"

He is not my blood but how have I connected with him so deeply? Is it God? How is a stranger from a foreign country without a doubt my father? From the first minute we locked eyes to the last minute I looked in his eyes, the word Daddy has been a strand that has tethered us together, never unleashed. Love has no DNA or blood binding us together.

"Isn't it a beautiful day? It just makes me want to go to the mountains, Pooh."

7

We sit on the patio and look out at the large open field behind the house. July in Oregon is gorgeous with bees buzzing and the familiar sound of a chickadee.

"Ooh did you know there are blackberry bushes over by the other yard, Daddy?" They call us back to memories of Soap Creek Valley when he was still living on the property on which I grew up. "Do you remember your daily walks to the blackberry bushes on Soap Creek Road to find loads of yummy blackberries?"

He laughs. "Those were some sweet ones, weren't they, Pooh?" Treasured now are the moments that seemed so trivial at the time.

His eyes flicker while his 88-year-old body is warmed by the cloudless sky and his mind dreams of the walks and moments we shared over the years. There is an unshakable knowing that this is our last moment slipping away. He turns and stares at me. The storied flashy eyes I knew as a young girl shine like diamonds.

My sad voice breaks the silence. "I have to go, Daddy."

"Oh, okay, Pooh. It is so nice to see you today. You are still pretty. I bet the boys still come after you," he chuckles.

Meandering through the door and onto the sidewalk, I hear what sounds like a jack hammer beating out of my chest. This is the moment I never thought would come so fast. One of my God-given talents—or curses—is knowing things before they happen. Saying the last goodbye sucks.

"Okay, it's been wonderful to see you." We hug and kiss on the cheek.

What is it going to be like to "not" be his daughter anymore? My throat catches and chokes me. I hug tighter and manage to hold in what feels like a runaway trailer truck of emotion gaining momentum, about to run over anything in its path.

"Bye, I love you."

He grabs my elbows, looks into my eyes. "I love you, Pooh."

In a quick retreat, I turn and head to the car. I glance back to see Daddy turn with his walker and head towards the front door. I succumb to the sobs.

"Warrior is there to remind us to be strong. Do not fight through the pain but rather, *breathe* through the pain by grounding our feet in and being aware of what is real now. All you need is your breath to keep living and experiencing a life lived. Each breath floods the body of cleansing oxygen and brings us to a fresh new perspective and different point of our life," Kelly continues.

As I try to complete my next breath, I imagine his last. Standing firm in the knowing that he was my dad and that the land had nothing to do with our timeless love for one another. There are gifts of real love that occur spontaneously in life without a thought. These gifts stay with our spirits and our hearts during and beyond a lifetime.

While in my sweaty Warrior II pose, the memory of the snicker on my dad's face fades into the wall that I am staring at. I decide to no longer fight for it, to give in, and let things happen without trying to control anymore. He showed me it was not worth fighting for. I decide to be strong, soft, and let go.

SACRED TREE
पवित्र ट्री

I WISH THEY WOULD JUST STOP WITH *the damn high push-ups, low push-ups, and downward dogs and do something easy. I just want to scream! Matt's half New York accent and his god-awful attempt to sound Indian is annoying as hell! Oh crap, he just noticed my pissed off look!*

"Ooh, I am getting the dirty looks now! It is okay, you can either change your perspective or stay stuck!" He says as his eyes pierce through me.

Shit, these damn big Indian eyes can't hide anything!

"Let us come into tree, bring your hands to heart center. Bring the right foot to the inside of the left thigh and ground down to feel your firm foundation on one foot. Breathe in deep and breathe out. Practice Ujayi breath. This means in through the nose and out through the nose. Focus on a point in front of you as you practice Drishti: A gentle and focused gaze at one spot in the front of the room," Matt says.

I smile knowingly. *I love this pose! I am strong on this one!*

"The breath is what connects you to that greater part of yourself. It stops the anxiety and brings calm to your nervous system." Matt says. His glance with a smile acknowledges my smile.

"Close your eyes and reach up, expand your tree as you open your heart to the sky. Allow yourself to grow taller in your tree." Matt continues.

The grounding woodsy aroma of cedar floats into my imagined tree. The Deodar, or cedar, means "timber of the Gods" in Sanskrit. The cedar doorways of sacred temples open like arms to pull me back to India.

"Open your heart even more and bend back to where you can see the back wall of the room." Matt continues. I bend backwards as the phantasm of the village of Mussoorie unfolds behind my eyelids.

I love daydreaming about India. I can feel a spirit and rhythm to life there that I can only feel while in nature in the United States.

This place is comfortable: no smog, no crowds in December, and I take long walks on steep hills. International boarding schools stand proud on hillsides. Students from all over the world come here to study in prestigious boarding schools. I come here to spend time with extended family: Mummy, her husband, Champa, Robert, Kamal, and Scott.

I am so glad to get out of that god-forsaken city!

The three days in Calcutta are a distant memory. The only remnant left is the stuffy nose and sore throat that clings on. We survive the harrowing thirty-hour train ride through the fertile fields of Northern India and up the Ganges. We are here to see my cousins and extended family that live here. It is the second day in the mountains at the breathtaking "Queen of the hill stations." Mussoorie is only fifty kilometers from the China border and surrounded by sharp jagged peaks covered with pine trees, oaks, shiny birch trees, and cedars.

An abundance of trees root themselves into the steep hillsides above the massive Doon Valley. The majestic mountain village wins my heart with its gigantic cedars. As I progress on my walk, the mirror images of the cedar trees from my childhood are at every turn. I spot one that is familiar. *I love that tree.* Mama D transplanted one in our front yard as a sapling from the forest of its family so it could grow for our pleasure. I treasured it as a symbol of my adoption from India. It was one lone tree, plucked from its home and family, expected to survive all by itself.

The air is crisp, dry, and fresh. The mountains that give me peace in Oregon are halfway around the world but I am inspired in the same way here. I am close to God—or whatever that thing is I find in nature.

In the morning, Robert, Mummy, and I take a walk along the village roads and slide along patches of ice. The sky is bright blue with small wisps of white suspended high above. It is one day until Christmas and Mummy is stopping at every church to pray. She does not care what faith the church is but only that she prays at every doorway. She is bent over touching the step to the entrance of each church while she mumbles in Hindi. Her love of God is palpable.

"God at all church," Mummy says.

This is the longest sentence I have heard from her!

We stop at a church, and she points the way in. No stained glass windows. No statues. No pews. A small table at the front with plastic flowers and a holy text opened is the only hint of a church. Four rows of tightly placed folding metal chairs support only fifteen people who are sitting and staring at the foreigners. Robert and I creep around the others in hopes of melting into a chair. Mummy gestures for us to sit.

"You foreigners." Mummy smiles. She is proud of the fact that we are foreigners and people stare at us.

"What the hell are we doing here?" Robert says to me.

"I have no idea," I reply.

The service begins. The minister is a dark gaunt Indian man with a sweater and dress pants on. No robes or priestly garb.

"This is a Christmas service," Robert grumbles as he rolls his eyes. He hates religion. He hates a lot of things.

"Yeah, I guess. We do not even go to church for Christmas at home," I laugh.

"Your mother thinks we are Christian; she is doing this for us," Robert whispers.

"I don't understand a word. They are doing the whole thing in Hindi," I reply.

They carry on about Jesus, Mary, and Christmas. *I know those words!* It is a small service but identical to any Christian program in America I have been to.

"Even in India, they love Christianity," I say with surprise.

After it ends, we file out and everyone smiles at us. The I-just-went-to-church-smile, the one I have seen in countless churches in the United States, graces the faces of these parishioners.

"*Calō calatē hai,*" Mummy says as we stumble out.

I have figured out that means "Let's go."

This time we meander down the opposite side of the village street. She is stopping again at every doorway to any church. She stops, bends over, touches the ground in front of the doorways, and does *prārthanā,* or prays.

We walk past the shops full of heavy wool clothing. Mummy bunches up her fingers and takes them to her mouth as if to eat.

"You *Khānā?*" Mummy says.

"I think she is asking us if we want to eat," Robert says in my ear.

"Okay," I nod my head and reply to her.

I look up to see an outdoor vendor with dead chickens hanging. They are whole and some have feathers, some do not. They are also alive in cages waiting to be beheaded and die. I hate seeing this; it reminds me of Mama D killing our pet chickens or rabbits and then making us eat them. She never told us until after the first couple of bites. "Oh, that is Babe the cow that tastes so good today. I guess it's all the good alfalfa we fed her."

Mummy stops and points to the cage with chickens; she talks in Hindi to the man. She picks a chicken from a cage and the guy kills it right there on the spot.

I stand stunned. *That is a little too fresh for me!* (Later, I find out the chicken is special for us, and they don't eat it often because it is too expensive.)

With our little plastic bag holding a dead dinner chicken, we make the long, meandering, steep hike up the hill that brings us back to my cousin's house. Shortly, the cousins and their kids disappear. Mummy and I are the only ones left at the house. We do not know what to say to each other. She grabs a plastic chair and puts it in front of the open doors in the sunshine.

"*Baiṭhanā.*" Mummy says as she points to the chair.

Oh, she wants me to sit with her.

She grabs another chair and sits next to me. The double doors to the house open inward to frame the deep plunging hills spilling into an endless valley below. We sit looking out the doors. Time stands still. We are one mudslide away from slipping to the bottom of the world.

I stare at her. I stare at her fingers as they clasp her hands together and then raise my gaze at the red streaks on her hair. Her body shows physical strength with strong shoulders and arms. Her face is serious without even a hint of a smile. The tiny, pierced jewel on her nose twinkles in the sunlight. We gaze into each other's eyes. Her eyes speak of yearning, hesitation, and frustration as she struggles for words to begin talking. An embarrassed smile arises as the language of Hindi falls between English words.

Unspoken words are lingering between our two spirits. The words dangle tempting us to find lines of communication. The connection comes through a glance or a subtle facial adjustment, hand movements, minimal words, and through an almost telepathic communication from mother to daughter.

I look out to see nothing but blue sky and mountain peaks off in the distance. Nothing else can be seen even though we were surrounded by a village of houses hanging all over the steep hills around us.

Trying to peel away the layers of years that had come between us, I continue to study Mummy's eyes, skin, hands, toes, ears, cheeks, and mannerisms. She is beautiful to me.

I finally see myself in a woman, another human being. We have similarities. She clasps her hands in her lap just like I do. She seems physically strong but soft, just like what others have said about me. She is small in stature, shorter than I am. She looks so tiny as she sits and begins to open her mouth to speak.

As we gaze into each other's eyes, it feels as though I am reading a book. A book that shares a deep sorrow. She speaks words without a word. Through those soft subtle facial expressions, I follow her spirit to a place of truth. The truth of who she is and who I am. There is no hiding from her intense and penetrating gaze. Her childlike shyness peeks through the skin on her face.

She is reading me too! She is mesmerized by me too!

"You my baby," she speaks as her face now sinks with sadness.

A wave overtakes my body. It is as if the earth moves, and my body is shaking and vibrating slowly.

"Yes, I know," I reply as I hold back the tears.

The critical voice in my head races with thoughts of denial.

How could this be my mother? She looks so young, so beautiful, and not old enough to be my mother. How does she even know for sure that I am her daughter? Why didn't she love me or want me? Why did she send me to America?

As I lean forward more to look into her eyes, I can only see sadness and a deep yearning to communicate her innermost thoughts and feelings.

"You gone very long time," she says as her eyes pool with wetness. She points to her heart. "I your Mummy. You my *ek* baby," she cries.

I remember that "ek" means "one" in Hindi. I hold my index finger up. "Your first baby, yes. Yes, your first baby!"

It is a baptismal moment for me, something so beautiful washes over and rinses away a hurtful label, the motherless label I put on myself. I breathe easier. My chest opens and my heart feels free.

"You small baby, so sweet." A smile sparkles on her small face.

Until now, I didn't know what I was like as a baby. There were no photos and no one to recollect. I had always thought I must have been a horrible baby if my own mother didn't love me or want me. I had pictured myself as a crying, screaming, demanding baby that my mother gave up on.

"You: Mummy, Mummy, Mummy and cry, cry, cry." Mummy giggles.

She has fond memories of me crying! I'm elated. No one ever shared an experience of me as a baby.

It is so strange to hear this woman I barely know remember me as her baby. In one sense, she is an absolute stranger. That is why I look diligently for similarities. In another, it feels so natural for her to be my mother.

My mind is still having difficulty wrapping around this notion. *Is this really the woman that carried me in her belly? Okay, so she holds her hands the same way, her mannerisms are reflections of mine, and the deep sadness that oozes from her pores and eyes is a definite mirror image of mine.* Because I have been motherless for so long, I chose to forget anything that had to do with a mother/daughter relationship between us.

As she stares into my eyes, she softens more and smiles a warm smile connecting us even more. She lifts her hands and turns them from palms facing down to palms facing up.

"You small baby, my baby, you go." She speaks. "I don't know, you go."

"You don't know where I go?" I find myself talking in broken English now too.

"I don't know you go." Her face lights up knowing that I am understanding what she is saying.

"No, no, Pushpa. Your small, small shoes, your cloth, but no Pushpa." A tear trickles slowly down her cheekbone. She is so heavy in the heart. It seems I have finally seen someone who has a heavier heart than mine.

"I love my baby, Pushpa." She cries.

The words pierce my heart and break open my deepest emotions. A flood of feelings buries me. The tears start.

But she didn't love me, she didn't want me. That is what Mama D told me!

As I look at her face, an even stronger, more rational voice commands my attention.

She is not lying. Look at the pain in her eyes. How can you deny this woman? She has nothing to gain by lying.

The idea of being unloved by my own mother was now just a pile of senseless words. I begin to rejoice in my mother's love as I start doubting Mama D's words.

"You go away America. I don't know America. Rabeya tell me you go to school, to Madras." She struggles with the words, but I am listening to her broken English and studying her bodily expressions.

A flood light of truth suddenly comes on! "Oh my God, you think I go to school in Madras?"

"Yes, Rabeya, she take you America." She continues to cry. Her forehead wrinkles. Her face looks full of pain and guilt. I feel light-headed. "Rabeya tell you, I going to school in Madras?" I ask.

"Yes, yes. She very bad lady," She answers.

She keeps looking at me between sentences. She is studying me also. She looks like she is also in shock that she is here looking at me, telling me her story.

"I go Madras. I take," she says as she grabs at her neck and earlobes.

"I looking and looking Madras school, and no Pushpa."

"You went there looking for me?" I say excitedly.

"Yes, long time you no come house. No holidays," she replies.

"You sell your necklace and earrings to go?" I ask.

"Yes," she cries. She nods her head between sobs. "Yes, Rabeya, no nice woman, she tell me you go America. I pray, pray, pray for you one day to come." She grows quiet.

The sun is now getting warmer as my realization sets in. *My life has been one big lie. My mother never gave me up. We were both victims. How could Rabeya have been so calculating and cruel?*

We spent the next hour looking at each other in awe of what we were experiencing.

"Your American family nice?" she asks.

"My family okay, Mummy not love me, Mummy not nice," I tell her.

A look of disbelief and worry saturates her face. "Oh no, your mother, Shirley, not love you?" she sadly asks. "No, not good Mummy, no love me."

My mother grows sadder. She is realizing that my life with an adoptive mother has been painful.

"Good daddy," I say as I smile. I want her to feel good about my life even if it was not the best. I can see the worry on her face when I tell her "Not good mommy" so I want her to know I was okay.

"Your daddy Thomas, no nice. He hitting me," she says as she points to me and then her belly.

"He hit you when I was in your stomach...pregnant?" I gesture and question.

She nods yes. This is a shock considering I have been told Thomas was wonderful and almost a God-like man.

"He was very cheating man," she reveals.

The conversation continues and I discover that Thomas and Rabeya were the ones who sent me to America.

This day has become one in which a bolt of truth knocks me off my feet and the reality of myself is changing forever. I am no longer the daughter of a perfect father, but the daughter of a mother who loved and yearned for me. She prayed for me to come back for years because she couldn't do anything else. She was the victim of a trusted friend and her husband. Somehow those prayers are answered. I now know that I am loved.

I'M PACKING MY BAGS TO go home, and I reflect as I pack. Everywhere along this trip, I have seen the sacred Banyan trees gracing the countryside of India. I love that tree because I relate to it. It is called the "wish-fulfilling divine tree" and it symbolizes eternal life. The conversation with Mummy in the kitchen revealed to me how *I* am the Banyan tree. That conversation began a journey of planting a seed just as the Banyan tree does; it grows another root that sprouts even more roots, eventually creating an entwined myriad of separate trunks forming what looks like one tree. It creates its own support system, a foundation of self-love that continues to sprout new roots.

I came to India to find my roots in the country and the culture but now I realize I found more than I ever imagined I would. By discovering the love of a mother and the reunion with my Indian culture, I became one with myself. I recognize that my American family was part of that root system. A mixture of cultures from the East and the West makes my base even stronger than if I were to choose one or the other.

Like the sacred Banyan tree, I, too, have separate trunks from separate roots forming one tree.

Poinsettia Doll
गुड़िया

"Pushpa, you are Indian and fit. You should teach yoga. You would have such a great following just because you are Indian."

Oh yes, I can be the next yoga Guru! (Insert eye roll.)

These things have been told to me since yoga started becoming more popular here in the South. Today, I step into this yoga studio and meet Kelly; I am immediately challenged.

That first time I tried Baptiste style yoga, which is really just hot yoga for Americans who have that need to pump up their bodies, I only did it to get me out of my rut, to break some boredom and challenge myself with something new. I had tried Bikram yoga. It is another very hot yoga that holds 26 postures with very little movement and is a good workout but I found myself getting bored with it quickly. It is predictable and monotonous after a while. That Southern spring day when I began the yoga journey, I cannonballed out of my comfort zone as I stepped into the studio and got checked in. The teacher, Kelly, took me upstairs and showed me the studio. The high ceilings and tall windows overlooking the tops of palm trees with a backdrop of blue sky and white clouds made me feel at ease.

The echoing New Age music, familiar from my massage therapy days, also brought a sense of comfort. The women and a couple of guys were lying down on their mats relaxing to the music.

"I am thinking about teaching yoga. Everyone thinks I should because I am Indian," I say with pride to Kelly. With her sharp country accent, Kelly quickly snaps back, "A person doesn't have to be from India to teach yoga, anyone can do it." Surprised at her response, I gulp down my large ego and say, "Oh, yeah, you are right." I wandered off to adjust my mat.

On the outside, I stay composed. The inside, however, is a different story. *How does this white, blonde woman with a twangy Southern accent think she can say that to me? After all, she is teaching something that came from the country in which I was born. How can she even think she can be a good yoga instructor when she doesn't have an ounce of Indian blood in her?* I am a little put off by her indignation, but I go ahead and do the class.

According to Mama D, Southerners were lower than everyone else, the bottom feeders of our class system. Indians, however, were the "most intelligent race with more class and culture than anyone else." Mama D would exclaim, "They *must* be poor and uneducated, just listen to that god-awful accent those people have," as my father would quickly pass through the channel playing *Hee Haw*. "You can't even understand that they are speaking in English!" Mama D loathed everything the deep south seemed to stand for: "that twangy country music, the uneducated-sounding vocabulary, the ridiculous bigots they all are, and the trashy women." Because Mama D was an educated, fair person who believed in people and equal rights for the "Negroes," I grew to believe this was all true, that she would never say something against anyone unless it were the truth. The people of *Hee Haw* did seem a bit like country bumpkins, and I thought maybe she did have a valid point.

Mama D didn't even like describing people as black and she loathed the "N" word. She talked of her father and how he hired "such nice Negroes to work for him on his hop ranch and never called them niggers." There were only a smattering of other races in my schools: a Chinese or two, a Mexican or two, one or two American Indians, a couple of black people, and maybe a couple of us East Indians in a high school of hundreds of kids. Racism didn't show itself for there were not many to be racist against.

After the first class, I am hooked on this type of hot yoga, but I keep battling a gnawing, little, judgmental voice: *Why have you been learning yoga from white men, a man from the Dominican Republic, and now in a studio in redneck Jacksonville with a Southern woman? None of whom have spent their lives being yogis in the Himalayas!*

A piece of me questions: *Who are these people and what am I doing learning something that should come naturally to me? I am Indian. I have been to India. I have family in India. Why am I learning something so ancient, so indigenous to my homeland, from people who have never even been to India or studied in India? Shouldn't I be finding my yoga master in a Himalayan village in Northern India? Better yet, aren't they supposed to just appear when I am ready? That is what all the spiritual books say,* "When the student is ready, the master appears."

Even on my trips to India, I had hoped for the master to appear like the magical stories I had read but nothing ever happened. I never fell onto my guru who was waiting for me to be ready and knew that I would one day arrive. I conclude that I am not worthy of a master yet; I am not ready for them.

"WITH A NAME LIKE THAT, yoga should come naturally," another class member says to me when we introduce ourselves. I shrink with insecurity as I'm once again faced with the reality that I am not the enlightened Indian from India who I should be. I haven't lived up to the expectations thrust upon me by others who think I should know all there is to know about the Indian culture. I am just another

American in search of a hard-core workout. Yet, I'm also searching for something more, something greater than this existence.

How the hell did I get here, in search of something that should have been mine? Why did I have to be thrust into this culture and forced to learn about the culture I came from instead of living it?

I nod to the classmate and mutter something insignificant to get past the awkward moment. It works.

Three Months Later

I think I have finally gotten over my prejudices of this Southern country girl teaching *me*, the girl from India, yoga.

I love her style. Kelly is a badass instructor but leads the class as a life coach. She pushes us past physical weaknesses with her inspiring and uplifting bits of truth that penetrate my heart, causing me to break down emotionally at times. Within those breakdowns is where I find truths about my own life. There are emotions, fears, worries, and memories I continue to hold onto. They keep me from living life fully and being present to the gift that life really is. I can't stop liking Kelly even though in my head, I hear Mama D say, "Those people from the South really are so ignorant and backwards in their thinking."

After months of yoga classes, I am struck by the realization that my mystical and magical expectations of a guru search are unnecessary. My journey is happening now. Multiple teachers bring tidbits of truth into every class and guide us to move forward in our lives. I don't have to go to a holy city or temple halfway around the world to find someone to guide and lead me through my quagmire of emotional baggage that stagnates in my body. I am healing here, in a place that I have historically loathed, by people who were the last people I would look to for a pathway to enlightenment.

For the past three months, I have been attending yoga three to four times per week and I am beginning to feel like this will never get any easier. Every day it is a new practice with something different to tackle physically and mentally. Today seems more difficult than ever.

"One more deep breath in and twist a little more," Kelly says cheerily as if it is so enjoyable for us. "Then come into rag doll. Feet wide open with hands on opposite elbows as you bow to the earth, hang here and let the head drop, get some rest in this pose."

My hamstrings and feet cramp while I am "resting" and this truly feels like torture. My gaze goes between my knees to the back row of the room in an attempt to catch my breath and relax. There are two young gentlemen and three thirty-something, slightly over-weight women all bent over in rag doll. It is a sea of all white pale skin hanging out of tiny spaghetti-strapped tank tops. The men are white too. As I take my gaze around the room, I realize that, again, I am the only one in the studio who is not white. I am an Indian girl in an alabaster world. I quietly giggle to myself and realize the irony of me being in this room learning yoga. In three months, I have seen less than a hand full of yogis who were any other ethnicity. The intense loneliness comes as I see myself isolated and separate.

"Drop your head even more as you drop your thoughts," Kelly says. "Mmm, this feels so good," she continues.

As the blood fills my head, I try to drop my thoughts and close my eyes while I focus again on my breath.

"LET YOURSELF BE LIKE A Raggedy Ann doll," Kelly says.

Anger comes bubbling forth as I hear Mama D's voice in my head say, "You were just a little rag doll when we got you. You were small and adorable, just like a doll."

I did not like being called a rag doll. I didn't have red hair, white skin, or freckles like my Raggedy Ann doll, but she told me I was one and she bought me doll after doll after doll. For a hearty and calloused woman, Mama D sure enjoyed the softness of a doll; they represented the girl she wished she could have been.

"Drop your head even more as you drop your thoughts," Kelly says. "Notice how good this feels..."

As I hang there, I melt into the scent of the Christmas tree standing proudly in my childhood living room. The tinsel is hanging and falling to the floor. Our red and white fuzzy wallpaper with crests and flowers accented between stripes is the backdrop. Poinsettias fill our home. The large windows look out over the valley of damp brown fields and the darkness of winter shows on the hills as the empty trees reveal only trunks and leafless branches. Steel gray, ominous skies with not a hint of sun for weeks hang over the valley.

I am ten years old and a fresh new American! A new tradition in my life is opening presents on Christmas Eve and believing that Santa comes the next morning to my house on a sleigh led by Rudolph. He comes down my chimney bringing me presents and a stocking filled with an orange and a little gift, like a comb or brush and Chapstick. *I'm pretty sure "Santa" is really just my mom.*

It is Christmas Eve, and we are ready to open the presents. I am excited. The voice of Andy Williams softly swoons "bright copper kettles and warm woolen mittens" over the scratchy old 33 record. The presents are wrapped with paper from last year and placed under the tree with large chunks of haphazardly ripped masking tape holding them together. I begin to poke and prod at the gifts to see if I can find the Malibu Barbie doll I so badly want. There it is! The box is the same size as the one I saw in the toy section of the Fred Meyer store. I am elated! I am now going to be like the other kids with my new Barbie doll. I can't wait to get my hands on it. I lift up a section of wrapping paper and peek; the box says "Barbie" on it, so I know I am definitely getting the doll I asked for!

Christmas Eve is when Mama D wraps most of the presents hastily, only minutes before we open them.

The typical frantic search for tape and scissors happens and then the bedroom door closes. Minutes later, Mama D brings the presents out with an air of obligation and plops them under the tree—with a heavy sigh—next to the presents I had just snooped through. "There," she says. "The presents are ready to open now."

I am posed and ready to rip open the package. My heart is racing, and my breathing is shallow; I just know that I will get the Barbie doll from the commercials, the one that all the girls want. The Sunset Malibu Barbie is really cute with her sun-kissed skin. She comes with a beach towel and a swimsuit; her long blonde hair and blue eyes top off the look of the perfect American girl who I so badly want to be right now. Owning her is the closest I will get to having that media-imposed all-American look. It might just bring me one step closer to being that which is so highly respected among my group of friends.

Mama D tosses my present towards me. "This one is yours," she says with a happy look on her face. Mama D is not much for presentation or surprises, so she wrapped the box making it obvious that it was a Barbie. I can't believe it. I told her how much I wanted Malibu Barbie and she actually listened! I was only moments from getting my doll; I could hardly stand the excitement.

"Go ahead and open yours first," Mama D says to me.

I stick my finger in the tiny hole which I had peeked in earlier and rip back the paper to see a "Black" doll with black hair wearing a nurse uniform. My happiness is shattered, and I feel like someone just slammed me to the floor from the sky.

"I thought her skin was close to the color of your skin," Mama D says. I want to scream at her: "I am not Black!" Too afraid to sound ungrateful, I devour the words before they can slip past my tongue.

"She is one of the few minorities on television that has a respectable job and speaks like she is intelligent," Mama D says about the doll that was made after a character on a series. Somehow, she thought I could find a piece of me in her Blackness, in her being a Negro, but I couldn't. I was deeply disappointed in that doll. I wanted a "real" Barbie, but Mama D insisted, "I thought she looked more like you than the other Barbies." Later, alone in my room, I threw the black Barbie in the back of my closet and hoped she would disappear into the darkness.

"RAG DOLL IS A PLACE to rest, to let the chaos of what we just did go and find some refreshment," Kelly says.

MY REFRESHMENT IS SOURED BY the memories of the Eskimo dolls, the "Native American" dolls, and any brown doll Mama D could get her hands on. She buried me in brown dolls when I really just wanted a Barbie, one like all the girls had to play with. Why did I have to be banned from the most popular doll, the blonde Caucasian Barbie? She didn't look anything like me, but I just wanted to be like everyone else. I wanted to play with the same things, walk and talk the same, and feel like the American citizen I was on paper.

In the 60s, there were no Indians anywhere. Television had just started having the "token Black people" followed by the all-black shows but there were no other races. The magazines were white, the movies were white, everything was white, and all I wanted was to belong by blending into the same way of living as the white kids.

I am not Black, Eskimo, or Native American. I am the "real McCoy Indian" as Mama D would say. She called me her doll, but I would not accept that I could be a doll. I never saw a doll that looked like me. Not even close.

As we come out of rag doll pose, my mind travels to a more recent time. My daughter is ten and I am elated to find an Indian doll with a sari; she is beautiful with long brown hair. I buy it for my daughter. It's the very first Indian doll I have ever seen.

"An Indian doll for you. She looks like you Kali," I say.

She plays with it for a while and puts American clothes on it. She takes the sari off. The Bratz dolls that look more American are her dolls of choice along with her blonde Barbies. Even with more cultural options available for her to see and experience, and having a mother from India, she still chooses what everyone else has, not the one that she can identify with as looking similar to. I am disappointed in her lack of interest in the Indian culture, but I realize why: she sees so little of it, just as I did, and thus we continue with the same issues over twenty years later. She lives in a white community with hardly any Indian contacts, doesn't know her Indian family, and lives like the all-American girl. I find that I cannot teach something that I am not.

I am an American in an Indian body.

Perfumed Daisy
सुगंधति

THE TINY WINDOW IN THE FRONT of the room is my focal point as I stand in the deep lunge of Warrior I. I breathe deeply as the burn in my thick thighs grabs hold of my mind. Outside, the tops of the palm trees seem to say, "Reach higher with your hands," as they point sharply towards the sky.

"Reach for opportunity. Create that space in your life and in your body. Spark your hands as you reach for possibilities," Kelly says.

I notice that my mind wanders from prayers to thoughts. *Please God, change my damn life. I am so sick of sadness and misery. Yeah, like God is really listening to me in a yoga pose! He never grants my dreams or wishes.*

Kelly, our instructor, encourages us. "Feel your roots and just take off. Come onto your right leg into airplane. Find freedom and wings as you dive in without a thought. Thinking is what gets in your way. Jump into the pose without a thought. Keep your spine straight with your heart lifted. Reach your hands to the back with the palms facing down. Feel free and rooted at the same time."

I look up at Kelly while she adjusts me; she has a big pink daisy on her tight tee shirt. The daisy jolts me to memories of coming to America.

"Focus a few inches in front of your foot keeping steady. Firmly root yourself on one leg and stay with intention," I hear Kelly say as my airplane hits wavy turbulence. I am nauseous.

My breakfast is coming up. I feel I am flying thousands of feet in the air without control of my own destiny. I close my eyes and breathe.

Please let's not throw up, not now! Let's keep my all-natural, gluten-free waffle with peanut butter from showing itself to the entire class!

I relive looking out a different small window. I am six years old, staring out an airplane window and wondering how this big bird stays up in the air. I look down at the city lights. Scratchy, rough, woven seats rub the back of my legs. This is my first time on an airplane. My feet dangle above the floor as I gaze through the tiny window at the clouds floating up and making me feel like we are dropping down. The window feels cold to my hand; it has the entire trip.

I am flying but where is it that I am going?

The clouds, they float in the air like my feet float as the plane slowly lowers through the blue sky and white puffs. My tummy tickles making me feel sick, but I try to not let anyone know as I hold my belly. I roll my round brown eyes back and turn my head to look across the aisle and see my neighbors with their mouths open and asleep. My other arm squeezes my new stiff, stuffed dog to find comfort. My dog is brown with fuzzy hair and can bark and walk if I push the button to make him do it. A crinkled brown paper bag holds a pink dress patterned with big fresh white daisies and a bottle of perfume, my first. The bag rubs my leg as the plane descends, swaying back and forth. The seat belt tightens on my tiny hips.

Looking around at the plane full of strangers, I am quite aware that I am all alone. People quickly perk up and close their mouths.

The flight attendant announces, "Fasten your seat belts and prepare for landing." We are arriving in Honolulu, Hawaii. As we come down lower and lower, I am scared.

I think about my mummy and one of our traditions. "Mummy, Mummy, can we have ice cream?"

"Okay, Pushpa you are always asking for ice cream every day."

I smile looking up at her with my hand in hers knowing that this is our time together. I love when we smile and giggle. We look at beautiful, elegant saris through shop windows and daydream about wearing "that one." The shop owner smiles and acknowledges my interest. "Your daughter, she has expensive taste," he nods to Mummy.

Then, the mango stand demands my attention. Pulling her hand, I start to head across the street. "Mummy, can we eat a mango?" The sweet fragrance of cut mango makes my mouth water. I have forgotten the ice cream and the dreams of being a princess in a sari. "Goodbye, see you next time," the shopkeeper calls. The memory fades as I fall into a restful state.

A hand taps my shoulder. "We are about to land," a voice softly whispers. A tall woman, with a perfectly coiffed hairstyle perched like a yellow beehive on her head, startles me. Karen, the flight attendant, comes to see if I am buckled in. I forget my daydream of Mummy and me. My tummy tickles. I don't know where we are, but this is the third time I have had to land on my trip. I am 42 pounds and standing a spindly three feet and five inches. My haircut is a chopped pixie with bangs straight across. I don't like the way the nuns had my hair cut off, but they did that to all the girls at the boarding school. We all had the same haircut.

The shiny orange booth seats that I made into my bed at the Hong Kong airport seem so far away: a faded distant memory. I am tired, sleepy, and worried.

What do I do now that the plane is coming down again? Is this the end?

Sleepily, I stagger as Karen walks me through the plane and then through customs where the kind customs guard says, "Welcome to America." I sit and wait for the next flight, my brown paper bag sitting next to me.

Hours later I am on another plane. My tummy feels sick. I feel the plane settling and coming in for a landing. My belly tickles again. Karen leans across the seat and rustles through the bag on the floor, hands a dress to me and says, "You must put this dress on so your new family can recognize you when they meet you. Their daughter will also have the same dress on." Karen smiles with every word flowing from her mouth. She is in her stiffly pressed, dark blue uniform. When I started this trip, she told me her name is Karen and she gave me a set of wings to pin on my dress. I wear them proudly and feel special.

Karen smiles and turns her head to talk to the other passengers across the aisle and I take the dress in hand. I sadly look down at my dress I have on. I like this frock. I don't want to take it off. I have been wearing this since I left home; my Auntie Rabeya gave it to me.

How can I still keep my dress on and not upset anyone? The dress that Karen wants me to put on is not soft. I am not wearing the matching bandana. I am not changing my dress!

I sigh and decide I had better do as I've been told. I begrudgingly push my hands into the armholes and push my head into the *unwanted* dress. It slips right over the dress I have on. I sit in my two dresses and look down to see the bottle of perfume given to me as a gift from a stranger along this journey. I pick it up and begin dowsing it on my hands; the bottle is difficult to manage with the large opening. I pour it in my hands and spill some on my legs, arms, neck, and on my face. It is almost gone so I dump the rest in my hands. I continue to pour and rub. The odor permeates throughout the airplane.

Karen arrives again. "What have you done?" she asks, wrinkling her nose and waving her hand in the air like a fan. The smell of perfumed flowers fills every inhalation.

"I smell like flowers!" I speak. The gentleman and older woman across the aisle smile and shrug their shoulders.

Looking out the window, pale yellow lights begin to appear quickly as we once again descend to the earth. The engine roars as the plane slows and the landing gear hits the ground. Multi-colored red and blue lights stream by as my gaze goes out to the dark sky. Droplets of rain bead on the glass of the window and drip as we slow down and taxi on the runway. Karen explains to me this is my last stop.

"Welcome to Portland, Oregon. The temperature is 38 degrees, and the time is 11:43 p.m." The pilot says.

Where am I? Who will be taking me from here? Where will I go?

Karen holds my hand as she walks me off the plane and down the long corridor to the gate. I like Karen. Her hand is skinny and boney; she smiles looking down at me and calms my racing heart. She carries the big blue teddy bear she gave me. He is soft and snuggly. I have the barking and walking dog under one arm and in the other arm, a dancing Japanese music box a man gave me in Tokyo. I am drenched in the perfume. All these gifts have been given to me along the way by strangers.

The smell in the air is damp and old, a moldy smell, one that is different and upsetting to my stomach. An inclined pathway leads me to a crowd of white people with eyes staring at each person coming off the plane.

Where are the people who look like me? These people all look like the nuns at the convent.

I look up to see a girl wearing a pink dress with white flowers, just like mine. She has glasses that look like the shape of cat eyes with brown straight hair that doesn't quite hit her shoulders and bangs, chopped straight across like mine. She is much bigger than I am. She is so white.

"There they are, your new family," says Karen. Her hand slips from mine.

I wish she could still hold my hand. Who is this girl who is dressed like me?

She ushers me to them. A large chested woman stands tall and smiles with her crooked light-yellow teeth.

"You must be Pushpa."

"Yes, I am Pushpa. I came all by my myself and I can count to a tousand and one."

"Well, hello Pushpa! One day you can count for us to a *thousand and one*," chuckles the lady as she corrects my pronunciation of a "thousand." "I am Shirley, this is Don, and this is Marie," Shirley says.

"Hallo," I say with my high-pitched Indian accent.

I like Don, he has black shiny hair like my papa. Shirley makes me uncomfortable, and Marie looks unhappy.

"Could you take some pictures?" Shirley asks Karen.

Karen takes a few photos of me with the bear she gave me and some more of all of us together.

"Those are some great photos of your new family," Karen says.

"What is that perfume smell that is so strong?" Shirley asks Karen.

"She is wearing a whole bottle of perfume a passenger on the plane gave her as a gift," laughed Karen.

They are laughing at me. I think I smell beautiful!

"She also has a remote-control dog and a music box that an executive gave her, and the teddy bear is from me," Karen tells Shirley.

"I can see that she loves the teddy bear already," Shirley replies.

"Yes, okay, I must go now." Karen says hurriedly.

"Thank you for helping her to get to us." Shirley gives Karen a quick hug.

"Goodbye now, I hope all goes well," Karen says. She slowly disappears into the crowd; all I can see is her tall blonde beehive hair going farther away from me. I hold my teddy bear even tighter.

Shirley gently holds my hand. "Let's take you home now." *Home? Now where are we going? Is this my new family? They look different from me. They talk different. I don't know these people, but Auntie talked about her friends in America.*

"You certainly do speak English very well," Shirley comments.

"The nuns at school hit us with a ruler if we don't speak English," I reply.

A silence falls as Don and Shirley look at one another.

Don and Marie don't speak much to me but Shirley talks if there is any silence at all.

"Let's get your things and go to the car so we can get you to bed," she continues.

It is dark and damp. The drizzle sprinkles on us and the fog hangs around the parking lot. The car is a long, brown rectangle on wheels. The seats are folded down in the back and a sleeping bag and pillow form a bed for me so I can rest.

The smell in the car is nauseating to me. Shirley said it was wet dog smell.

"We waited so long for you to come, and we are so happy that you are finally here with us."

Shirley continues yacking nonstop about my flight being delayed so long that they had to wait in the airport all day. I listen with wonder and shock. I am exhausted and don't have any idea where I am or who these people are. I cannot stop studying the way they look. They are old, they are odd, and they look peculiar to me with their strange mannerisms. Shirley has such big front teeth while she talks, and Marie just doesn't talk at all but stares through her glasses. Don just looks at me.

Why did they want me to come here so bad? How do they know me?

I lay down in the sleeping bag and feel like I am going to throw up. I cover my head to shut out the world, snuggle with my new teddy, and go to sleep.

A couple of hours later we arrive at the house. Don picks me up and carries me in his arms safely above the barking dogs. They are jumping up and sniffing me.

Shirley speaks with her sing-song voice, "Pushpa, we are home."

I sleepily look around while Shirley keeps talking.

"This is our house." Shirley closes the screen door behind us leaving the dogs outside.

"The dogs are excited to meet you, too, Pushpa."

The smell of this house is pungent, scents I am unsure of but they make my stomach feel queasy. The same smell of dog from the car joins the smell of dust inside my nose. Antique dining furniture fills the room we enter. I gaze around trying to get my bearings while Don carries me down the dimly lit, narrow, and long hallway to a bedroom on his right. I feel safe in Don's arms. He is kind and gentle as he slowly places me on the bed like I am precious. I already have a liking for this man. Shirley turns on the lights while I look around. It has a peppy, pink, Pepto Bismol shade on the walls with a beautiful, flowered bedspread cascading over the edge of the bed. The color is the same pink color as my daisy dress.

"This is your bedroom," Shirley says.

I don't remember ever sleeping in a bed like this before. It is soft, comfortable, and envelopes me.

The beds at the Loreto Boarding School were metal, mesh beds with a mattress and blanket, nothing like this. Don takes my shoes off and they help me to get ready for bed.

"Good night, we are so happy you are home," Shirley says, and Don agrees. Marie watches from the door. They pull the bedspread up around my face and leave me to rest lying under a blanket and sheet. My doggie and teddy lay next to me.

Teddy and doggy will watch over me.

"Good night," Shirley says again from the door, echoed by Don and Marie. I cover everything but my eyes, pulling the blanket around my face so I can see what is around me. It is too dark to see much.

"We will keep the door open a crack and the hall light on. I will be down the hallway if you need anything," Shirley whispers.

I glare at the huge window with the black shadows dancing on the other side. My eyes grow wider. I am scared.

Where am I? What is outside those windows? What is at my window? Is someone out there? Who is watching me?

I can't sleep. Shirley comes in minutes later and sits on the edge of the bed, the light peers around the half-opened door. Her face is shadowed on one half and lit on the other.

"You can call me Mommy, I am now your mommy," she blurts out.

I am so confused. *Why are you my mommy? What has happened to my mummy? I can't call her mommy. She is not my mommy.*

"Are you hungry? Let's go to the kitchen and get something to eat!" she exclaims.

Her hand reaches for my hand and pulls me out of bed, down the hallway, and through the door of the kitchen. We enter the big room, and she walks around one of four chairs surrounding an old, round, wooden table anchored by a large single pedestal. I notice the large window the table sits under is just like the one in my bedroom. A long countertop runs almost the full length of one wall. Shirley reaches in one of the many cabinets and gets out a glass for me, pausing for a moment at the antique wood stove which stands proudly in front of a brick section of the wall.

"There is your chair," she points. "Go ahead and sit down." Shirley pats at the chair while she says, "Go ahead, it won't bite."

She is in a white nightgown with pink flowers. It trails to the middle of her calf. I can see through it and see her panties.

I can see this old woman's panties. She has a big, wide bottom! I can't laugh!

Shirley reaches for a banana off of the counter while I maintain my composure.

She looks like a sister at the boarding school. She might be just as mean as the sister if I laugh at her!

She turns around and brings it over half-peeled and hands it to me. This time I see her large, saggy breasts through the worn nightie.

"We are so excited to have you here finally. We have been waiting so long for you," she starts again.

Why does this woman keep telling me this? Who is she? How does she know me? Where am I? How long am I going to be here? How can she know me? Am I in the right place?

As I bite into the banana, I look up on the windowsill to see there is a picture of me, the same black and white one that is on my passport.

I must be in the right place; they have a picture of me!

This relaxes me and brings me peace. The nausea and anxiety lift and I gobble down the banana. I finish the last bite and can hardly keep my eyes open. Shirley walks me back to bed. "Goodnight, Pushpa," she says as she tucks me back in bed.

"I will show you all of our animals in the morning, I know they can't wait to meet you."

I barely hear her as I close my eyes.

मैं मा ँ याद आती है *I miss Mummy.*

I WAKE TO A LOUD "cock-a-doodle-doo doo" from a rooster in the early morning.

"Time to get up and meet the animals, Pushpa," Shirley says as she peeks in the door.

Shirley helps me to dress in layers of clothes. She is putting socks on my hands.

"There, that should keep you warm. You won't be used to this cold weather after coming from India."

We slosh through the squishy mud as I slip and slide around the barn and yard. I fall down and Don wants to carry me over mud puddles and through mud now. It mists on us. It is cold and damp. I shiver and my teeth chatter. I meet the cow named Babe, the horse named Boy, the two dogs, a couple of cats, and the chickens who I immediately do not like. As we walk, I look at the hills surrounding us with the overcast skies above and the muddy ground under my feet.

"The animals are yours, too, Pushpa." Overnight I acquired a new mommy, daddy, and sister as well as dogs, cats, a horse, chickens, a house, and a bedroom.

YEARS LATER, I AM TRUDGING through Mama D and Daddy's big garage. The one that is for their motorhome, Daddy's lapidary equipment, and all of his hundreds of rocks he found while rockhounding. A high ceiling with an attic above holds my treasures in a cardboard box: gifts from strangers to a little girl traveling to her new home in America. I climb the ladder to the attic and turn everything over and around looking for my box. As I jump off the last rung to the floor, Mama D walks in. "What are you doing?" She looks at me suspiciously. I haven't been home for several years.

"I'm looking for my box. The one with my Japanese music doll, my dog, and my Teddy. You know the stuff I brought with me on my trip from India."

"Oh, that stuff. I got rid of it last year. Didn't think you wanted it anymore."

And you call yourself my mother? God, why don't you just tell me how unimportant I really am!

Mama D walks casually out of the garage while I stand there feeling defeated. There is nothing left of my monumental trip from India, nothing to show the incredible generosity. The bear had given me comfort, the doll had soothed me with its gentle music, and the walking and barking dog had been my closest companion. Those treasures given to me on the airplane trip had given me comfort for years. From the hands of strangers came items which I clung to during fearful times, and they had always reminded me to be grateful for the generosity of others.

Those gifts taught me an important life lesson: give to those who really need the simple things, just as those strangers had done for me.

Today, I am sad my precious treasures are gone but I appreciate that I still have the memories. It's a lifetime later and daisies still remind me of innocence, the smell of perfume brings me laughter, seeing a stuffed animal makes me smile, hearing a Japanese music box brings peace. And most importantly, I remember that people are the real gifts.

GLADIOLUS

फूल

It's a sweet, sunny, Indian-summer Saturday. My nine-year-old body is agile as I climb limb from limb to the top of our broad-leafed maple tree, my favorite place to find solace. I make my way to the top. Like a monkey, my skinny arms and legs wrap the smaller branches at the top as I hang out and look down over the peak of the house. Below sits a sturdy picnic table built by Mama D and Daddy. Down below, hills roll all around Soap Creek Valley with hints of yellow dotting maple trees, my fourth summer with this second family coming to a close. Happiness fills me as I spot the gladiolas Mama D and I planted in the garden; they were beginning to lose their bloom. This life still feels new. I still really don't have a connection with Mama D. Her voice sings out my name down below as she opens the screen door in search of me; she never looks up. I stay quiet. I am enjoying this independence and distance from my life down there. The air is fresh, and it rustles the leaves hanging over my head, tickling me. She goes back in, never figuring out where I am. I giggle with pride in my ability to hide from her.

This is my place to go and be above it all, away from the pain I feel every day for being the daughter that Mama D says my mother didn't want. "Your mother didn't want you or love you, that is one of the reasons we adopted you," Mama D would boast.

The tree swayed as I enjoyed the warm, fall air.

I'm brought back to my surroundings by yoga teacher, Matt's voice. "Close your eyes and bring your hands up. If you want a little more challenge, go back for a tiny backbend."

My eyes close as I reach back and wobble while I recenter on my breath. I go deeper into the pose and slip back into the giant maple tree on the state property next to ours in Oregon. The climb is a more difficult feat than I am used to, but I am always up for it. As I confidently climb to the highest point where the winds blow and bring me to the edge, I hang onto the last branch. At the very top, I spy over the expansive fields of ecru: dry, tall grass blended with oats. It smells of the dry summer we are exiting. The earth has hardened and dried and so has the summer's flowers and trees. As my gaze falls to the old pioneer homestead below, I wonder how much this tree has witnessed during its lifetime. The sunken grave sites, the partially standing barn, the keg in the ground next to the creek to keep the pioneers' food cold all seem insignificant in comparison to the expansiveness of the land, valley, and enclosing hills. I feel insignificant and small. I hide here, hoping to stay forever but knowing I can't because Mama D is looking for me. I begin my descent.

"Come back and bring your foot down. The great thing about yoga is that you get to do it again with a totally new perspective on the other side. So, let's do tree on the left leg. Hands at heart center and let's do it again but fresh and new." Matt's voice is soothing and encouraging.

My left leg is struggling despite my intense focus on my breath and practicing *Drishti*, a Hindi word for staring at one place. A sweet smell of blooming summer roses drifts into my memory as I slip back into my tween years.

"THE ROSES ARE IN BLOOM," Mama D comments as she bounces on Old Red's black pseudo-leather seats. "The trees we planted near your property line are taking off and they're really going to give you a barrier between your house and the neighbors," she boasts.

As the 1964 "Old Red" Dodge truck crawls over the rolling fields through the three-foot-high cow parsley and the occasional oat stalks, the line of trees emerges. The property line is sharply defined with perfectly spaced Douglas Fir trees.

The rains have subsided early this year in the Willamette Valley, and we are facing the beginning of a seasonal drought. The hills look more like the end of summer in August than the middle of June. It is dry; the colors of green are beginning to fade to beige.

As we get closer, the hill of my property becomes more prominent, and I picture my house jutting out and looking magnificent with its contemporary architecture and expansive windows that face all directions bringing in a spectacular view to every room.

My days have been filled with hours of drawing floor plans for this house that I was dreaming about in my head. Drawing and redrawing my "house on the hill" were the beginning of aspirations to be an architect. I sketched it repeatedly while I sat at the French Provincial desk in my room, floor plan after floor plan.

"Your property really is the best piece because it has such a great view. It just needs some shade trees and shrubs so it won't be so naked and then you can have privacy from your neighbors," Mama D rattles on. "Yes, it is looking much better with the plants we planted the last couple of summers." Mama D happily rambles with a crooked smile. "The knoll where you are going to build your homesite will look so much prettier with the plants we have already planted. The lilacs, roses, and trees will make such a difference. I know it doesn't seem like it now but all these plants will look big and pretty around your house." It is summer and the chores include watering the plants on my property. As we make our way down the bumpy dirt road, the large barrels of water we are hauling are sloshing and spilling out over the top. We approach the end of the line of trees standing at attention. Mama D brakes and even more water sloshes out towards our back window; she laughs.

As I push the heavy door of the truck open, I realize I am only at the beginning of this long and tedious job. I sigh deeply as I see there are more trees to water than I remembered from last year. Mama D pulls the hose out of the back of the truck. She is rigging up the hose to "siphon" the water out of the barrels, so we don't have to carry bucket after bucket. "Let me fiddle with this hose while you start carrying buckets of water to the trees; here is a bucket, get started," she orders me. She throws me a plastic gallon container and continues working on the hose. The tailgate comes down. "You are just going to have to carry water to each plant. Make sure you don't waste any," Mama D continues ordering. "This is your land, and you will be living on it, so you have to take care of your plants and trees."

My skinny, small frame struggles as I climb up onto the tailgate. I carry water to the first tree, spilling it on my shoes. "Well, there's *one*. Keep going because we have a lot to do!" she barks impatiently.

I find myself watering tree after tree while she continues trying to find an easier way. Never finding it, she says, "I will be right back, I need something from the house. Stay here and keep carrying water." I continue as I watch her walk down the valley, over the hill, and out of sight. She finally returns after what seems like a long time—just as I am ready to collapse from exhaustion.

The only thing motivating me is knowing that, one day, this will all be mine.

It's later in the afternoon and I'm noticing a sadness I can't seem to shake. I know it's from the memory in yoga class earlier. I'm annoyed that what my sister did still bothers me. In her later years, Mama D complained, "We gave that land to her so she could live near us, and take care of us but I can't even get her to help me at times."

Initially learning that my sister sold the land, *my* land, was a significant hurt. My dream had been shattered but worse than that was realizing I essentially have no family. Then, this hit me over the head like a Billy club: inheritance was not going to happen. I considered myself ostracized from the family after hearing Mama D say, "I want someone in the family to keep some of our land" but yet it went to my sister. I took it hard that I was no longer part of the family and wondered if I ever really was.

Over the years, the sting of that hurt changed to a dull ache. My energy eventually shifted to my Indian family, and I learned that family isn't defined by land or inheritance. Family is about supporting one another, loving each other, laughing together, caring for one another, and really showing up as a family member.

I also accepted some responsibility in our family dynamics. I realized I couldn't show up fully for Mama D, therefore she never fully showed up for me. By distancing myself from my adoptive family, I inadvertently refused those family bonds. (This is not just an anomaly of adoption but a virus within biological families as well.) They never truly knew me, and I barely knew them. The truth is that I participated in the separation by not fully embracing the gift I had in my adoptive family. The outcome of that choice was isolation and separation and I was still on the outside until the day she died.

Despite our lack of a mother-daughter bond, we became "friends" over the years. When she died, I planted gladiolus in her honor, in memory of all of those she had planted with me. I watered them, just like she taught me. No matter how much I watered and cared for them, though, they died.

DAFFODIL
हलका पीला रंग

"TAKE A DEEP SQUAT WITH YOUR feet to the outer edges of your mat. Place your hands straight in front of you and bring your knees into your armpits. Look forward as you come into an arm balance called crow." The insecurities of not being able to do what other yogis can do rise as I give up and look around the room to see everyone else upside down. I am different just like always, the only Indian in the room and I can't do yoga.

This position zapped me with a deep emotional surge that reminded me of myself when I was on the verge of young adulthood.

I was a victim. A victim to a man. A victim of depression and of self-loathing by the hand of a loved one. It was a beautiful spring day in late May. I stood outside after a Sunday short shift at the local hamburger stand in town. In my greasy, smelly, brown polyester uniform with bright orange and gold stripes down the front and a zipper the length of my body, I stood in the parking lot and fell into the dreamy green eyes of a twenty-year-old boy. His wavy brownish blonde hair flipped at the neck under his red baseball cap. His wide, almond shaped eyes drew me in, and his charm had all the girls talking. His cheeks were slightly rosy, and he smiled a big smile that would warm even a cold damp day in Corvallis. I was seventeen and within days of graduation. Spring fever was bursting with Mama D's favorite flower: daffodils blooming at every turn. They brought with them a promise of new life, new beginnings, and a turn to adulthood.

We talked for an hour or so before we heard a big boom. Later, we found out it was Mount St. Helens erupting. However, not knowing what it was at the time, we went on with our flirtatious dance. His charm and intelligence oozed, and I became enamored. As it came time for me to leave, he asked, "Would you like to come over later?"

Without hesitation, I replied, "Sure."

He was a regular customer. All of us who worked there knew him and looked forward to his kind, relaxed, and intelligent conversations. I quickly drove home, changed, and came back to meet him. Although it was a Sunday evening, I was not concerned about school because I was about to graduate from high school in a couple of weeks. I found his little apartment through the alley and knocked on his door nervously and excitedly. He answered and then opened the door. He invited me in. It was a downstairs studio apartment in an old house made into apartments just for college students. I walked in and saw a girl sitting on his bed. There was no couch and the only place to sit was on the twin bed. We were introduced and then she got up and nicely walked out as he ushered her through the door.

The room reeked of marijuana. I knew that smell well because I smoked pot as much as I possibly could. We talked for a while and then he offered me a "bong hit" to which I happily obliged. I loved to smoke pot even though it made me paranoid. We listened to Tom Petty and the Heartbreakers on his turntable. The stereo became louder and louder after each bong hit and the walls of the house began to vibrate. We smiled through the puffs of smoke and began to connect over songs and smoke rings. He was cute and I was interested. I left and we began the courtship and dance of lust. He worked as a surveyor for the Forest Service in Oregon and made a decent living, but he wasn't in college, nor had he gone to college. That made me think twice about getting too serious.

Mama D always said, "You are so smart that you need to marry a professional: a lawyer, doctor, or engineer who is bright, or you will become bored." Her words kept rewinding in my head and my education snobbery was apparent against Ben. He was uneducated and not planning to go to college even though he was very intelligent.

I moved out of my house after graduation that summer and found myself stuck for two weeks between my rental and dorm without a place to live. I vowed I would never go back home no matter what. I was still seventeen and about to begin college.

Ben had now become my boyfriend over the summer. He heard my predicament and offered, "Why don't you stay with me?" It was a dumpy little run-down studio with a bathroom he shared with another tenant, but I figured it would be bearable for two weeks before I left to go live in the dorms.

He was serious about our relationship and I was not. He took me to his hometown, a seaside town in Southern Oregon and walked me through his favorite State Park with flowers in full bloom and told me, "I want to marry you one day in this park." I was touched but screamed inside, "I haven't gone to college and this guy's not a professional!" I was carried away by his charm and romantic flair, but I was just not as into him as he was into me.

In the first week of staying with Ben, we had loud, passionate, orgasmic sex continuously throughout the nights.

I decided I would have my mother meet me for lunch one day and she could see where I was staying for a few more days. I wasn't quite ready for Mama D and Ben to meet yet. I planned for her to come after he had gone.

That morning Ben had the day off so we had wild sex in the position he seemed to like best, me on top. We had an hour before my mother's arrival. After a few bong hits and with the music of Pat Benatar's *Heartbreaker* shrieking, we were in a heated sex session with the bed rocking and banging the wall over and over. All of a sudden, I hear a knock on the door and Mama D's voice say, "Pushpa?" The door comes open near the foot of the bed and Mama D walks in, greeted by Pat Benatar singing her heart out. She turns around as she realizes what she has walked into and begins backing out the door with a small, embarrassed voice, "I will be back in a while, I am going to park the car." The door creaks and closes behind her.

I freak out. "I can't believe she just walked in on us!"

"It is her fault, she should have come on time or waited to come in," he points out as he walks away butt naked to the shower. I am left in bed—humiliated, embarrassed, and scared of what Mama D will say.

Ben is in the shower for a few minutes and Mama D comes back.

"Yoo-hoo, are you ready for me?" She barges in the door again. I lie in bed not knowing she would be back so quickly. I am still naked and sweaty from the heated moments before. She comes over and sits on the edge of the bed and says, "I didn't bring you all the way from India for this."

I was confused and speechless. *What? Was I not supposed to have sex because I came here from India?*

She never spoke another word about it, not at lunch, not ever again. I was left wondering what she meant by that.

MONTHS LATER

I started college twenty miles away at a small college. I lived in a dorm in a single room and shared a bathroom with two other girls. One of the girls, Janey, asked me to go for a drive with her in her chocolate brown 1967 Mustang. I liked her and loved her car. She was making a trip to Corvallis, my hometown, so I thought it would be fun to go with her since I knew my way around and she didn't. I could help her.

We had an enjoyable drive there on a beautiful Indian summer day and I asked her if we could stop and say hi to my boyfriend, Ben. She was a sweetheart, always so warm and full of fun. She agreed but said we couldn't stay long because she had to get back and study.

I directed her to his dumpy little apartment through the alley and we parked. She kept the car running and sat inside it beside the front steps leading up to his apartment. I knocked loudly so he could hear me above the bass beating out Ted Nugent's, "It's a Free-For-All" on the walls. He answered the door.

"Hi, I thought I would just stop and say hello. I don't have much time and Janey is waiting for me in the car." He looked in her direction and flashed his big teeth at her. She waved back. I turned to leave.

"Okay, got to go. See you this weekend!"

He looked at me, his eyes piercing through me and said, "You are not spending the night?" I quickly replied, "No, I need to go. I don't have my car." He looked right into my eyes and slapped my face hard with his left hand. I began to cry.

"I can't believe you just hit me!" I turned and looked at Janey. I was humiliated, shocked, and walked away.

WEEKS LATER

An apology showered with love, kisses, and promises followed by passionate cannabis-high sex brought me to my knees. I went back.

Anger filled his actions when one night I dropped the bomb on him that I didn't think we should date anymore. "What are you talking about?" His rage spread like a Santa Ana wind-driven forest fire as he came across the room. I stood against a wall as he came and grabbed my long hair, pulled it, and then began to bang my head on the wall. I started to believe I was going to die. He hit my head so hard over and over that it hurt, and I screamed violently.

A knock came at the door. He ran to the door and looked out the window. "It is the fucking upstairs neighbors," he looks back at me displeased. He turned and opened the door with a fake smile. He knew how to turn into charismatic Ben—his outdoor personality. "Hi," he says. All the months I have visited here, I never saw or met the lesbian couple upstairs. Now, they were at his door. One of them looked around the door at me as I frantically sobbed. "Are you okay? We heard screaming down here."

I find an opening to get the hell out of this nightmare. "Please help me," I cried. She grabbed my arm around the door and pulled me outside. "Do you want to come upstairs?" I am afraid to leave for fear that Ben will become more enraged, but he keeps his outdoor personality and says politely, "She is okay." She looks at me and says, "What do you want? You can come upstairs and talk if you want to." I get a backbone and say, "Yes, I want to talk." She grabs me and holds my upper arm gently as we slowly walk up the old unpainted stairs to her front door. I begin to feel like I may collapse. My head is pounding and the reality of what just happened hits me as I begin to sob again uncontrollably. As the door opens, the sunlight showers through the wall of windows as the hanging spider plants suck up the rays. The wooden floor creaks as we walk to the overstuffed chairs. As we converse, it is as if a light just came into the darkest part of my life and woke me to the truth. "You cannot go back to him," she compassionately says. "We could hear you screaming and the pounding on the wall even over the stereo." I am embarrassed but also relieved that someone was here to save me.

I don't know how much more he was going to keep beating my head into the wall. For days, I would feel the bruises as I brushed or shampooed my hair triggering flashbacks of the days before.

For the next few months, he stalked me at school, showed up at my front door and threw rocks at my window on the third story apartment building in the middle of the night. A restraining order was issued but it never stopped him. He "loved" me. He was allowed by the police to harass me at my door as long as he didn't come in the room. There were nights of calling the police repeatedly. They forced him to leave but he would return immediately after the cops left.

Ben enrolled in the same college. He knew I didn't want to be with him because I had told him, "I am going to college, and you don't want more for your life." I ran into him at school. My adoptive older brother had just moved back and was also attending college with me. We had a tight relationship. Ben had never met my brother, Jeff. He is six feet four and rather intimidating with his authoritative voice but to me he is a puppy dog. He is sweet as can be and we had a close bond even though he was twelve years older and never lived at home. He had already been through a couple of failed marriages and the Navy but was starting over now. He was back living with my parents and going to college with me.

We fished and drank beer together, spent hours talking about life, and took college classes together.

This day we were walking on campus to class and Ben spotted us. "Oh my god, we need to go. There is that jerk, Ben." Jeff replied, "Where? I am going to get that asshole." Just then, Ben sees us. He walks over with intention. "Are you sleeping with him now?" He says smugly. Jeff loses it and begins to take his backpack off to get ready to begin fighting. Ben begins to do the same. I am caught in the middle. "This happens to be my brother you idiot!" I say loudly. The room is filled with students changing classes and we are the center of attention now. I stand between the two walls of testosterone and say, "Stop it right now! This is my brother dumb ass!" Ben says, "Oh, sorry." He turns into his outdoor guy again. Mr. Congeniality speaks with a big fat smile, "I am sorry man." Jeff turns and grabs his pack as he says, "Leave my little sister alone." Half an hour later Ben is crouched by my car ready to flatten my tire. As I approach, he sees me coming and flees like a nasty irritating crow that has been stealing food from a picnic table and does it with an arrogance and pride in being obnoxious.

I never saw him again. He stole the piece of me that was naive to physical abuse from a lover. I had never even been spanked.

MUCH LATER

I ate crow as I told Mama D in her old age, "You were right, I didn't come from India to do this. I am worthy of much greater. Someone who respects me and thinks I am special." She replied, "I always knew you were special, that is why we adopted you."

Cow Parsley
गाय अजमोद

"ROCK AND ROLL LIKE A CHILD playing three times and on the third one, come into boat," Matt says.

We are a room full of adults rolling back and forth on our backs. I stop and come up on my butt to get into boat pose. This is about the most childlike thing I have done in over thirty years.

"The body is in a 'V-shape' with the chest lifted. Be careful not to sink your boat by cutting off your breath and collapsing. A sinking boat means no breath and not coming from the heart," Matt says and looks right at me while lifting his chest.

As my boat is collapsing, I close my eyes and breathe. I quickly find myself catching my breath as I transcend to my first experience with a boat: the first warm summer in the Soap Creek Valley. It is 1969. The sky blasts blue and the gigantic fir trees covered hills embrace a fresh July day. The terrain is blanketed by a shade of dry khaki with white Queen Anne's lace dotting the fields like big snowflakes. Purple thistle-like plants are sprinkled intermittently amid a summer day. The yellow legal pad with the list of chores was half finished. "You can finish the rest tomorrow," Mama D exclaims.

The list was long, but we had both worked on it since 8 a.m. to only get partially finished. Summer included a list of chores every morning and a wake-up call before 7 a.m. to ensure "you can't be lazy" as Mama D proclaimed.

The morning had been filled with my side of the legal pad of chores including vacuuming, dusting, and helping to clean horse stalls. Shoveling shit was an ongoing job in the chicken house, in the horse stalls, and in the cow stalls. Marie and I spent many a weekend morning with shovels and pitchforks cleaning.

For some reason, Mama D was giving us a break this morning. She had a song in her voice as she proudly sang, "Kumbaya my lord, Kumbaya. Oh, Lord, Kumbaya."

"I bought you girls two new boats to play in so let's take them to the creek and you can float down to the bridge," she says in her fun first grade teacher voice.

Marie smiles at me as we both forget the hours of work we just grunted and griped through. We both run to our rooms to change. "You will need to wear something you can get wet in," Mama D yells happily. My heart races with excitement while I imagine the fun we will have in our new boats. Life had just gone from hell to fun in a matter of moments and we were due for fun.

Sitting on the lawn, a hard blue plastic boat awaited each of us. Marie's was a bit bigger than mine but both just big enough for one person to sit in.

We scrambled to grab them and began our trek to the creek. Mama D carried one end of mine as I clutched the other. She walked so quickly that my feet were stumbling to keep up. I was seven years old, about 48 pounds, and as skinny as a twig. The stinky snowflakes of cow parsley flowers brushed my shoulders while the thistles poked my legs. Marie was way ahead of us tromping through the field while I was being dragged by the boat and my mother. We came to the old oaks hovering over the creek and walked down the slippery bank to the slow meandering water. I sported my first floral hot pink bikini with a pair of denim shorts. It was too large for my small frame, but the colors were vibrant.

"Mama, are we putting the boats in the water?" I ask as my heart pounds loudly.

"Yes," she replies as I swallowed my heartbeat.

"You go first, Pushpa. Marie can come behind you," Mama D says.

The water gets faster and louder as it rushes over rocks on the other side of the creek while my heart beats louder and more rapidly. A few large maple leaves float by in the stream around the boats while Mama D holds tightly to both of them. Her polyester tomato red pants are rolled to her knees while her floral scarf holds her short, partially gray hair back as she stands in the water up to her shins.

As I look down the stream to see where the water is going, Mama D says, "Okay, you can get in the boat now." She holds the side as I gladly take my ice-cold feet from the water into the wobbly boat. She giggles and I shiver from cold which draws out the chills of fright from my insides.

"Okay, Pushpa, here is the paddle. Paddle on this side if you want to go the other way" she shows me while pointing. I practice putting the paddle in the water.

"I am scared, Mama."

"Okay, you are ready to go!" she exclaims with joy. She lets go and I slowly begin to flow down the creek. She wades out of the water and begins to help Marie with her boat. I look back to see her slipping farther away while she smiles and speaks through her semi-yellowed buck teeth, "Stop when you get to the bridge." A wide curve comes, and I lose sight of Mama D and Marie.

Fear sets in.

I am not smiling. I am scared to death. I don't know how to paddle or how far the bridge is from here. The vines of plants are hanging from limbs and scratch me as I slowly maneuver around and down the narrow creek without any control of which direction the boat is pointing. The boat is spinning around in slow circles while my worries spin on how I am going to stop at the bridge. Mama D and Marie are gone around the curves behind me. The fear is mounting as I drift alone in the middle of the silent creek. I can't hear their voices anymore. Enjoyment does not come as my heart races, and I only want to stop at the bridge and get out.

The boat swirls around and I notice ahead there is a fallen tree leaning over the creek with only a small area to the right big enough to go under the tree with me in the boat. The tree gets closer, and I don't know what to do. I find myself quickly at the tree without room enough to duck under. The tree bumps my body as I try to duck and lose control. The boat turns over and I fall in. I am not a swimmer. I don't know how to swim! I lay in the water with my head under while I look around at the rocks and small fish swimming around me. A crawfish backs up on my right as I fear the fish are going to eat me. The water is ice cold as my head begins to ache. I think I will die. The fish will eat me, or I will never come out of the water. I hear very little sound.

Some time lapses and I resign to dying in the water. Two arms grab around me, and pull me out as I begin to sob. It's my new sister Marie; she has her arms around me and she carries me out of the creek and up the bank. She is only twelve, but she has the strength of an ox. I cry and I cry as she carries my limp, wet body out of the bank of the creek and onto the rocky dirt road winding up the hill to the house. She is barefoot, wincing while walking on sharp, jagged gravel, "It's okay, you're okay," she consoles me. I sob from the depths of my body as the fear pours out. The sound of my uncontrollable crying soothes me.

MATT'S VOICE STERNLY BUT CALMLY pulls me back to boat. "Lay back pulling your arms overhead and your feet straight out, then come back up to boat again."

With all my might, I go back and come back up holding my breath and force my body into boat while putting my attention on the yogi's foot next to me. She has a large foot with perfectly French manicured toenails while the entire top of her foot bursts with a bright bold orange marigold tattoo. The colors are fresh and vibrant.

"Hold your boat but pull your heart up to the sky. Lead from your heart, see if you can find something fresh in this boat," Kelly speaks kindly.

I can't stop looking at the tattoo. The color of orange is so bright that it pulls me in, the details of the petals of the marigold bring it to life and allow the pungent smell into my nose bringing me to the Ganges River in India where marigolds beckon me for the search for spiritual experiences. "Take a deep breath in and a deep breath out." Matt says as he breathes deeply with us.

I CLOSE MY EYES AND drift in my boat to Haridwar, one of the seven holy cities on the auspicious Ganges River where small banana leaf boats of marigolds float.

My senses are elevated to the foothills of the Himalayan Mountains. Swaying to and fro in the Indian version of a Land cruiser SUV, the upbeat Bollywood music fills my ears with a haunting feminine voice praising the Ganges River and the many Hindu Gods. The language of Hindi that sounds so familiar and the spiritual essence pouring through the *Tablas* (Indian drums) shoots right to my soul and filters through the cells of my body and the core of my being. I am immediately transformed into the Indian me who can walk the hills of the Himalayan Lake region village of Haridwar and gander at the Ganga River with boats of marigolds floating while feeling the pulse of the heart of this place.

The day started at six in the morning after a couple of days of festivities of Diwali. Three days here began to become oppressive while a cloud of particles heavy in pollutants hung after the festival of lights of Diwali. The night sky was filled with fireworks and celebration for Ganesh and Lakshmi *pujas* (prayers) to bring prosperity for the new "fiscal" year. Ganesh, the mighty elephant god, removes the obstacles while Lakshmi brings forth the prosperity.

My brother Kamal, Colleen, who had come with me from the United States, and the servant Shama, and I drank gigantic bottles of Kingfisher beer while we ran for cover from falling debris under exploding fireworks to celebrate this holiday. The next day was layered with smoke from days of fireworks and the usual pollution of the diesel cabs and buses. We were chomping at the bit and raring to leave the city of Delhi and its choking smog behind. We were ready to go to the mountains and see the holy sites. Colleen, my ex-hippie chick acquaintance, was dressed in the native garb of a kameez with bangles adorning her arms while I sported tight denim jeans, a T-shirt, and platform shoes. This was her first trip and my second to India, ten years after my first visit, and we hardly knew each other.

We had only met twice in a metaphysical retail store where she worked before. She had asked, "Would you mind if I come to India with you? It has always been a dream of mine to go there." I didn't think twice and said, "Sure, why not?"

Colleen read about Reshikesh and could not wait to get there to see where the Beatles were known for visiting. She had a loud, boisterous laugh that penetrated through me and purged the laughs right out of my body. She wanted to learn laughter yoga. I said, "You should do something with that laugh," and two months later she was on a plane with me. I didn't even know her last name.

WE WERE LOADED UP IN our black Toyota Scorpio SUV, the Asian version of a Toyota Sequoia but much smaller, with our handsome

Indian driver. My mother in her traditional saree, Colleen with her big blue eyes and big blonde hair in an Indian outfit, and me, the Westernized Indian woman with short, highlighted Halle Berry hair, climbed in the back while Kamal rode in the front seat with the driver. We happily waved goodbye to Delhi as we went through military armed guard checkpoints while traveling north towards our destination of Reshikesh. On our way, we would go to Haridwar: a holy city with a temple my mother wanted to take us to.

Six hours of sitting with over-stimulated eyes wide-open watching buses filled to the brim, rickshaws made for a family of four people packed with entire extended families like sardines, bicycles pedaling trailers filled with crops, Muslim villages of black eyeless Birkas, and a sea of never-ending perplexed almond eyes staring in the windows while traveling to the holy city of Haridwar known as the gateway to God.

The traffic made no sense, and it was a free for all. Honk and move or be moved as we darted and dodged everything coming at us and around us. My waist was a couple of sizes smaller from the hours of constant gut wrenching and writhing during the long, slow, and treacherous drive. This might have been the "Gateway to God" but it sure was hell getting there. It was sort of a metaphor for life.

Colleen and I feared for our lives during the ride and were happy to unclench our jaws and get out of the car.

This small village is where the Ganga River comes from the Himalayas and spreads into the plains over the fertile soils. It is a place of ancestral salvation. Millions come here every twelve years for an auspicious festival.

The sun shone bright in the early afternoon with not an ounce of pollution to filter the rays. The Ganga River was clean and clear, not at all dirty and polluted. Surrounded with steep mountains that dive into the valley, the Ganga cuts its path and welcomes Hindu pilgrims to its bathing ghats.

Once we parked and peeled ourselves out of the car, my mummy started on a mission. Whenever a temple comes within range of her, she becomes this indestructible force to be dealt with. She led the journey as we crossed a long bridge lined with emaciated bodies perched at our feet on the left and right. Hundreds of endless eyes met mine as we walked for an eternity across the bridge. Each person had tiny tin pans for us to drop rupees in but I was afraid to leave any. With hundreds of people begging, I was worried I would start a line of people following me. Each spirit looked desperately into my eyes in hopes of any change dropped from our hands for them. We reached the other side with unbearable sorrow as I tried not to focus on the skeletal figures in my vision. There were too many to help any of them...*where do you start and how can you leave anyone out?*

Shanti, Mummy, charged up the hill to the cable cars that would take us high above the village to the temple for a puja. The gondola swept around quickly and stopped as we stepped into it. It took off as quickly as it came. Challenged by the speed and height with which we were climbing up the mountain, I prayed for our safety. The mountain was steep and the river quickly grew distant below us. We reached the top and my palms were sweating.

At the top, the spectacular view of the wide, clear Ganga cutting its way through the valley beckoned me to come back down to the village below, but we had to go into the Mansa Devi temple. There is a statue perched there of the goddess who fulfills desires. We tied a red string to a tree and Mummy finished our pujas. We were soon back on the rickety old cable car sweeping down the mountainside back to the village. Still following Mummy, we walked full speed to keep up with her back down to the bathing ghats by the river.

The village was filled with people coming for the rituals and also for pilgrimages beginning here. There were not many other people from the West, mostly Indians. Mummy purchased three boats made of banana leaves filled with fresh, vibrant, gold marigolds and a candle to place in each vessel. I was as clueless as Colleen, and I looked on not knowing what Mummy was doing with the boats of marigolds.

She handed one to each of us and instructed with her hands to follow and said, "You come." We obediently followed. Carrying my boat, I looked down and smelled the fragrance of the flowers. I began to feel as if I had smoked pot, on a high similar only to marijuana highs. We followed Mummy's sari down to the edge of the river where concrete steps lowered down into the river. She pointed down to my platforms and said, "Shoes, here". Slipping our shoes off and to the side, Colleen, my mother, and I carried each of our boats down by the concrete stairs leading into the Ganga. Mummy lit the candle in hers and said a puja in Hindi for herself. Then, she gently waded down the stairs into the water as she held the banana leaf boat up and then released it into the river and watched it slowly drift down with the current. She turned and waved to Colleen to come into the river, said a puja for Colleen and waved for her to go into the flowing current and release her boat also. We watched as her boat went from side to side and had a rough sailing. Then, she came to me. Not knowing what she was saying in her pujas, I did as I had seen. I waded to my knees in the great Ganges and released my boat. She watched as the boat smoothly sailed with no bumps. She smiled and told me, "Very nice, you have a lucky life and find a good husband." She was happy about the way my boat smoothly flowed with the river and said, "You very lucky."

A man with wide eyes and a big grin looked at me as I put my shoes back on. I asked Mummy, "Why is he staring?" She didn't have time to answer. He spoke to Mummy in Hindi and then came over and handed me his small baby, a boy that was crying and crying. I knew he would stop crying if I held him. He stopped immediately as soon as I put him on my hip. I held him and they snapped photos of the baby and I together and then photos of the whole family with me. Colleen and I were perplexed at why. Later, I asked my mother why they wanted photos of me and not Colleen (she is the blue-eyed, blonde American) and my mother replied, "Because you very lucky."

Three months later, I did meet a man. Many people prayed for me while I was in India to get another husband. I did but he ended up being an alcoholic. The prayers did come true. I did have a husband. When you don't pray specifically, you never know what you are going to get.

My boat came in and landed as a container ship with healing, lessons learned, surprising forgiveness, travels to amazing destinations, a home, and a heightened passion for life but also separation, loneliness, and growth.

As a small child, the boat brought me fear and drama. While as an adult, the boat brought luck and hope of getting closer to God at the gateway to God. It is in our own perceptions of our reality that hope, or desperation come. Even in the smallest of situations.

CHRYSANTHEMUM CITIZEN
गुलदाउदी नागरकि

THE SWEAT IS POURING PROFUSELY AND the old man next to me keeps blowing his breath all over me. I just want to grab him by the neck and scream through a blow horn!

Don't you know your breath stinks?!

"With feet wide, come into rag doll. Keep the knees bent, grab the elbows with the opposite hands as you lengthen the spine and bow forward. With your peace fingers, grab the big toes and come up to flat back, inhale and bow forward and exhale. Make your breath loud and support each other by letting others know you are here through your breath," monologues Kelly.

Oh, believe me that old guy is definitely here!

My wet, old, wrinkled peace fingers want to flip off the old guy but instead, I have to choose peace.

Can't get pissed off during yoga; that would be sacrilegious.

As I battle in my mind to find peace in the present, I escape to 1972 when the peace sign is as popular as the present-day cell phone. They are on T-shirts, on patches sewn to ripped up old jeans, and on stickers stuck to VW vans. I love the peace sign and so do most of my fourth-grade friends. Big stickers of peace signs and McGovern cover my sea blue notebook.

Who the hell is McGovern?

The pride of placing my hand on my heart while doing the Pledge of Allegiance to a country I love was my favorite part of the day.

Nixon is running for his second term in office against McGovern and the Vietnam War is raging while I show off the silver bracelet of a man that I have never met who is missing in action.

Veterans pour back home, one wounded man after another displaced in society with missing parts and tragic hearts. I am deeply moved by the news images of men on crutches and in wheelchairs. As paradoxical as it may seem, this was the year this little dark child living with white folks became a true American patriot.

It is an early morning wake-up call from Mama D who chirps songs like that of a spring robin outside my window. Her whistling is incessant, and her Suzy Sunshine routine has become monotonous every dark, cold, and damp morning. Even on this special morning, I want to hide my head under the covers and tell her to shut up and go away!

"You will finally be ours," Mama D cheerfully exclaims.

The bed squeaks as I roll over annoyed at her. The creep of the morning light hasn't even begun to float through the window.

"Get up and get your clothes on. We are going to court today," Mama D says.

I did not sleep a wink. This is my big day.

Today, I get to miss school and go to the school that my mom works at instead. I am relieved and excited. I am going to be the center of attention which scares the shit out of me. Her class is taking a field trip and going with me to get my citizenship today.

I wait until Mama D is gone and then I get up. My clothes hang on the doorknob as they do every morning. I put on a bright red blouse that frames my face with ruffles and tuck it into my cotton home-sewn skirt. Mama D made this skirt for me, and I am madly in love with the mini red and blue Chrysanthemums that cover a navy background. The suede blue clogs that have been a hit with my fourth-grade posse of girls slip right on over knee-high socks. I am confident in this outfit. I glance in the mirror and smile at my patriotic look.

I will be an American citizen today!

Mama D forcefully brushes my mid-waist length, dark brown hair into two long ponytails. She finishes it off with a fat, bright red, fluffy yarn bow tied at the base of each ponytail. I am officially American with my red, white, and blue and ready for my big day.

"You are so lucky we adopted you and saved you from that horrible life in India. God knows if you would even be alive today if you lived there." Mama D says while she glances at her face in the mirror.

We have our usual breakfast of fresh, warm cow's milk, straight from Babe's udder and jiggly, sunny-side up eggs that make gagging a daily morning occurrence.

"I can't eat," I say.

"Drink at least one swallow of your milk and eat some of your egg. You were so malnourished when we got you and I just don't want your growth to be stunted." Mama D says sternly.

Why can't somebody just put their arms around me and tell me I am going to be okay?

I am more nervous than usual.

Am I going to have to get up in front of everyone to get my citizenship? Will I have to speak in front of people?

My heart pounds like ferocious animals are after me and I am not sure whether to throw up or run in the bathroom and poop. I have a horrible fear of being in front of people even if I don't have to speak. I hold back a gag when I see the yellow yolk and envision the egg coming from the chicken's butt.

"At least a couple of bites and a swallow of milk before you can leave the table." Mama D says.

The steam from the milk rises from the top of the glass.

"That milk is so good; I just milked Babe this morning. Her udder has been a little raw lately but she sure is supplying us with plenty of fresh milk. Drink some." Mama D harps.

"I don't know if I can." I begin to explain.

"I don't have time for this today." She complains.

Daddy and Marie are already finished and gone.

"I have to go get ready." Mama D says with frustration.

She pushes the chair under the table with a deep sigh and leaves the room.

Finally, the Wicked Witch is gone! Cue the Wizard of Oz music.

The old dog, Bobbie, is faithfully looking at me with the look of, *I can get you out of this one.* I quickly dump the eggs into the dog dish allowing the dog to gulp it up in two-seconds. I pour a bit of the milk into the bowl, too, because Mama D is happy as long as I have at least "one swallow" and now the glass would look like I had a swallow.

I got one over on that mean old Mama D!

Later, Mama D and I drive the back roads of the Willamette Valley to get to her two-room school. Mama D is full of joy and excitement. She grins as her front teeth, colored with bright red lipstick, protrude over her lip. I sit and sway from side to side along the winding pathway leading our way. Our truck, "Old Red," just chugs along up and down small hills.

"You will be ours after today. Until now, we always felt like you weren't quite our daughter yet." Mama D explains.

Why wasn't I their daughter? I have been living with them for years and they tell everyone that I am their "adopted daughter from India."

"Once you're a citizen, we won't have to worry about you ever going back to India. You will really be ours." She continues.

I listen.

No stranger in our path goes without hearing of Mama D's rendition of my adoption story. She says it with so much honor and dignity. She is so proud of herself for having me.

"I spent two years trying to get you and I am so glad that we are finally almost done. I am the one who wanted you. Everyone else thought I was crazy for adopting a poor child from India that I'd never seen." She continues with her story.

"I've proven them all wrong; there is nothing wrong with you."

Good thing my IQ test showed signs of being an almost genius.

"People told me you might be developmentally challenged or have a physical handicap but look at you. You are beautiful, smart, and you have nothing wrong with you. You know you really are so lucky to be adopted. You could have been dead by now or been married off. You should really be grateful to us." Mama D says all this without stopping for a breath.

Did she really save me from a horrible life? Why do I have to be so grateful? I didn't ask to be adopted.

We coast into the front of her red two-room school.

"They are here. The newspaper reporters are here with their cameras. I called the *Salem Statesman* to come and take some photos for the paper and to write an article about adopting you and going to get your citizenship today." Mama D yelps.

Oh God, I have to be interviewed and in front of a camera to get my picture taken? I hate getting my picture taken!

We get out of "Red" and walk by an unfamiliar car.

"That must be the reporter's car. I have never seen it before. I wasn't sure if they would come to take pictures for the paper or not."

The reporter looks up from the other side of the car.

"Hello Mrs. Deardorff, I am here from the Statesman."

"Great, so glad you are here. Come on in."

We hastily charge through the double doors and into the school.

The school is only big enough for two classes, a kitchen, and a boy and girls' bathroom. One side is my mother's class with first and second graders, while the other side has a room for the third and fourth graders.

As the door opens, the children all light up with smiles. They love Mrs. Deardorff and, even more so, love when she brings me. It is like being a new kid on the block every time I come here.

"Hi Pushpa! Hi Mrs. Deardorff!" Multiple kids belt out. They have been eagerly awaiting our arrival. Their field trip today is to go to court and see me get sworn in as a citizen and then go to the park for a picnic.

I am so loved and important here. I love coming here!

The children are surrounding me and all talking to me at the same time. They know me well from all the times Mama D lets me tag along to school with her. They are familiar with my occasional visits but explode with enthusiasm today. Mama D has a hard time keeping the kids away from me.

"Leave Pushpa alone, you can't all talk to her at the same time." Mama D says. The kids are louder than usual, but they listen to her and calm down.

"As you all know, we are going to the courthouse today to see Pushpa get her citizenship and then we will go to the park for lunch afterwards." She continues.

The roar of the kids breaks out in laughter and talking again.

Moments later, the reporter walks up.

"Mrs. Deardorff, I think this is a good time to take the photos. Let's do some before we go with all the children behind you and Pushpa." She speaks.

The children are ushered together as they are told to stand with Mama D and I in front with the children behind us.

"I think we should get the American flag in the picture." Mama D exclaims.

She jumps up on a chair and takes the flag down from the corner of the room. She hands it to me.

"Here, you can hold it," she says. I hold it awkwardly and proudly at the same time.

"Look at the flag and show how proud you are to become an American today." The reporter says.

I look up and puff up like a proud peacock.

Finally, I belong to this great country!

The reporter asks me questions but Mama D answers most of them for me.

We load up and go to court with a room full of kids. I am sworn in with twelve others. The only other Indian family that I have seen is here. We spend lunch at the park eating and playing. It is a fun day, and I am happy.

The Next Day

Mama D proudly brings me the newspaper with my photo on the front. I am happy. I feel important and special. The photo of us is front and center.

"Read the story about you inside: it is my interview and tells your story," Mama D says.

I open the paper as Mama D goes to the kitchen. I begin to read and feel an out of body experience as I read on.

This is all about me like I am someone different, someone who is worthy of all this attention. I am an American. My colors are red, white, and blue and I love the many stars on the flag. I wear red, white, or blue almost every day. Pink has faded from my clothes and now red stands out in my closet as the color of choice. The ribbons in my hair are red, my favorite blouse is red, my pants are striped like the flag. I ooze with American pride. I am American.

I read on: "Mrs. Deardorff says they found Pushpa starving under a house in India…"

I quickly scamper to find Mama D.

"The paper says you found me under a house, but I didn't live under a house." I say horrified. *I don't want people to think that about me.*

"Yes, you lived under a house. You lived under Rabeya's house." She explains.

I can't understand why she thinks this even though I repeatedly tell her that it is not true.

TWO YEARS EARLIER

The pop radio station has a contest and Mama D insists that I write my story to win. "Just write why you like school and you will win."

"That will be easy, I love school." I reply.

I sit at my desk and pour out a letter filled with heartfelt gratefulness and love for school, for learning, for my friends and my teachers.

"Look Mama, I am finished. I think I will win that contest!"

She glances over it.

"How do you expect to win? You didn't write your story about us adopting you from India and that you were starving and living under a house in India." Mama D retorts.

"I didn't live under a house." I reply angrily.

"You lived under Rabeya's house, which is what she told me." Mama D replies.

I begin to believe her and decide that she must know something I don't. I can't argue with her. My memories are already faded. I surrender to what she tells me and begin to believe it.

"Let me help you write this so you will win," she continued.

She grabs the letter and tells me to get another piece of paper. Let's start all over.

I sit with my pen and paper as she dictates my letter as to why I like school.

"I was adopted and lived under a house. I had no opportunity to go to school. I was poor and starving..." She dictates the entire letter.

I write verbatim.

The radio announces my win.

On the outside, I am the winner with my letter read on the radio but on the inside, I am angry for not really writing it myself.

THIRTY YEARS LATER IN INDIA

I am finally ready to see my home under a house on Russell Street. Ashamed that this is what I came from, I avoided seeing it before.

"This time I want to see where we lived. I want to see Russell Street." I tell Mummy.

"Russell Street, I show you. You were sweet baby there." She replies.

She happily meets me at the hotel and is ready to give me the tour of my old neighborhood and home. We jump in a yellow diesel cab and ride into the heart of the city. I envision the leaking ceiling and the dark apartment that was "under Rabeya's house." Looking out the window, my nerves unravel as it sounds like we are nearing the correct street.

Where are all the homeless people all over the streets? The hungry eyes flooding the sidewalks, the beggars?

Mummy gestures to the left.

"Russell Street, here, here." She says to the cabbie.

I am braced for horrific conditions that may unnerve me, that may flood my eyes with sadness, and that may make my gut wrench. Mummy points to the white high-rise building.

"The tobacco company," she says.

She points to the side of the wide street and gestures again more aggressively to the cabbie to pull over. Metal gates still stand from the last three decades. The street looks smaller than when I ran barefoot on these sidewalks. The gates are open as we walk through the narrow little street to the apartment building at 4 Russell Street. The building is a bit run down because it is now used only for commercial use rather than home dwellings.

My mother's young man friend, Caen, comes with us and translates.

"You used to live here in this apartment." He speaks.

"This one here?" I reply.

"Yes, and you would run up and down these stairs." Caen continued.

God, it is exactly how I remember it! Small, dark and downstairs from Rabeya!

I am having flashbacks of this place. Very vague are the memories but there is a familiarity. Mummy stops to chat with the men working. They are making flowers for a wedding. One man is outside sitting on the concrete in what looks like a central courtyard area. The building has a narrow central courtyard with a stucco style building around us like a U-shape. There are stairs going up behind the seated man. As my mummy talks with him, she is getting emotional. She is obviously telling him in Hindi that she lived there and then she pointed to me and told him details about me. She is talking and telling him her story of living there over 30 years ago. I begin to recall running up the stairs and visiting a man who lived up the stairs.

"Very nice old man live there," as she points up the stairs.

I nod my head as icky memories come into my mind.

"He babysit you." She continues.

Now it is so clear, the vivid memories as a child that I never understood. The visual of an old man with a wrinkly penis that was forced in my mouth had reeled in my mind over and over. I really believed that one day my new father would expect this also. I didn't know if it was bad or good: just that it was a part of life.

Breathe in and breathe out, I hear vaguely from the background of my memories.

Russell street was a real place. The place where I was a citizen of India. A place where I lived in the downstairs of an apartment building, not under a house. It was my home. However bad or good it was, I was with Mummy. I had a life in this place where I played with other children, held hands with Mummy, laughed with Mummy, ran up and down the stairs, served tea and snacks to foreign dignitaries, had an Aunty Rabeya upstairs that taught me how to make chai.

How dare the newspapers print that I lived under a house? How dare Mama D even tell people this regardless of whether it was true or not!

This place was better than some of the places I have seen in America that people live in. No one is judging them and saying,

"We need to save those kids from that horrible life and take them to another country to make their lives better." There are children in our inner cities or in places where they are not getting the education, the health care, the food, or the attention and love but no one is out to save them. Foreigners don't come here to America and see places that are obviously ram-shackled and decide to try to adopt those kids.

Russell Street and Calcutta is a part of who I am. The poverty, starvation, sexual abuse, and the lies still permeate in that run down, unused building today.

In seeing the truth, peace came over me just as it did when I held my hand to my heart during the pledge. Coming home as the Vietnam veterans did from the war with pain for a lifetime, I, too, carried the pain of a lifetime after coming home. There is no place like home but *what is home?*

I am now the lover of two countries, the citizen of one with the origin of another.

Champa Lei

चंपा

GROUP ORGASMIC SIGHS RELEASE FROM THE few of us that follow along with Kelly. Her natural beauty, blonde short ponytail, and eyes that come to a tiny slit when she flashes her wide, perfect, orthodontic straight smile makes her appear that she is not a tough girl but her classes are, in fact, very grueling.

"Return to this place, in downward dog. Breathe in and breathe out with a sigh, mmm."

God that Southern accent is so annoying! She sounds so backwoods! How the hell did some country girl end up teaching yoga?

"Lift your right leg up, bend your knee and reach for your neighbor while opening up the hip. "Mmmm" she sighs again while my arms quake to hold up my body in what seems like the fiftieth downward dog.

Kelly says mmm as if she enjoys this, but I'm irritated! I would enjoy this, too, if I was the one telling us what to do and not in the pain that I'm in!

"Now square the hip and step your right foot to your left hand for half pigeon to the front of the mat. Set it up with a block under your hip. Lead with your heart and with grace as you bow forward."

As graceful as I can be, I lean forward to bow to see the beads of sweat clinging to my chest. My forehead hits the floor while my palms come together reaching forward to connect with my spirit and quiet the mind through my breath.

"Come into pigeon with a choice to cling to the discomfort or choose to let go and cling to your breath. Breathing in and out through the nose, you can hold onto all of that gunk or let it go," Kelly continues.

My bow is going deeper, and my mat is pressing on my third eye. I imagine the sound of fluttering wings. I am transported to eight years old.

GAZING BACK FROM THE FRONT seat of our baby blue Galaxy 500 sedan, I see the dirty and rusty old bird cage in the back seat with the pigeon in it poking its beak through the metal slats and fluttering its wings.

I don't like birds. They are all chickens to me, just waiting to peck holes in my hand. Mama D kept homing pigeons in a cage by the barn. She loved the idea of having two of them, a male and female. She took them out every day so they could fly but they never left. She wove a love story about the two of them that seemed ideal.

"They have only one mate all their lives."

The two of them live happily ever after. Like Cinderella and the Prince. I fantasized about them having their own little castle.

"I find pigeons to be so interesting. Did you know that they always find their way back home?"

"Really?" I pretend to be interested.

"Yes, they were important in the world wars for delivering messages. They are really smart."

"How do they do that?" I ask.

"I am not sure, but they always go back to their home."

"You know Pushpa; we are giving this pigeon to the Goodling's. She is a homing pigeon, and she may come back."

I turn to look back at the pigeon, and feel sad to know it is being separated from its lifelong mate. I wasn't going to miss the pigeon but she was being separated from her friend. That is sad to me.

"She will like their barn just like our barn," Mama D says joyfully. "And the Goodlings will take good care of her."

Mama D gets lost in her thoughts. "You know Pushpa, my Indian friends told me that in India they believe that if they feed the pigeons, they will never go hungry in their next life."

Maybe I didn't feed the pigeons in my last life, I think to myself as I gaze out the window.

We count the days since we left the Goodling's. I am actually just as excited as Mama D to see if our pigeon will come back home.

"It has been forty-three days since we dropped her off."

"Do you think she will come back?" I ask.

As we stand by the barn, we watch the boy fly around swooping over the cedar tree for his daily flight.

"My goodness! He is flying way over the trees and going farther than he usually does. Hope he doesn't leave and get lost trying to find his mate."

We look up to see him coming back with another pigeon following him.

"I think she is back!" I shout.

"Does she have the ring on her claw that we put on?"

They flutter back to the top of the cage and land together.

"She came back!" Mama D announces.

"Is it really the same pigeon, Mama?"

"Yes, Pushpa, it's her. She flew all the way back from the Goodling's. Now you know homing pigeons really do come back home."

Why don't I ever want to go back to India? I wonder.

It is joyous to see them back together flitting from the barn to the chicken house together again. I can't stop imagining this bird flapping her wings for all those days to come back home following all the twists and turns of those country roads and back up our driveway and home. They were together again enjoying their homecoming.

TwENTY-TWO YEARS LATER, I GET the aerogramme from Rabeya in India. She was my only contact with my first home since I left.

"Your father has died in a horrible accident," read the letter. I went into a tailspin, drank excessively, and hardly ate. I cried over my biological father, the god-like man I thought I had wanted to see one day.

Months later, I see a psychologist and so-called psychic.

"I think we should do a regression and hypnosis session with you," she suggests. I agree.

Nothing happens.

I can't believe I just paid fifty dollars for that. I don't know what I was thinking!

I drive away and within two blocks the images come so clear of my father Thomas and his sexual exploits with me. I instantly realize that he loved me in *his* ways, like that of an obsessed lover, not a father.

I can't believe Thomas would do that to me. I am crushed. I can't understand how I idolized him all these years! *Why am I missing him? Why am I mourning him?* I am really mourning my home, India. I am going home. I want to see India. I want to see where I came from.

Over two years go by as I dump Scott—the man I thought would be my husband forever—for absolutely no reason and run to another relationship seeking comfort. After knowing my father sexually abused me, I kept it from Scott and left feeling unworthy of the love of my life. Not knowing why I left until decades go by, I grieve for the life I had.

I start a new life with a new man, Robert, and a new career. I am a massage therapist at a sweet little spa on the ocean. Daily, I share my story of being adopted from India with many clients and their response is the same.

"Your mother is still alive?" One of many clients questions me.

"Yes, she is still living," I reply, uninterested.

"Do you know where she is?" He or she says inquisitively.

"Yes, she is in Calcutta." *Oh God I have to let these rich snooty people in this spa know that I came from poverty!*

"You should go see her."

"She didn't want me, so I don't want to see her, but I do want to go see India!"

"Then you should go. How do you know she didn't want you?"

"My adoptive mother told me."

Great, now they know what a loser I am.

After months of hearing this from naked people on a massage table, I come home to Robert one day and express my desire to go.

"I want to go see where I came from."

"Don't you want to meet your mother?" Robert says puzzled.

Shit! Now I am hearing it from him too?

"No!" I say adamantly.

God he is bugging me about my mother also! Is something wrong with me because I don't want to see her? Maybe I should think about it.

"Let's do a ceremonial ritual and tie this sword that I got from my best friend Bob who died in the Gulf. It can be for the trip to India. I am going with you. We are going to see your mother. This may be your only opportunity to see her."

"Uh, okay. Fine." I reply annoyed.

He takes me upstairs to the sword and ties this cord intently around the sword. I don't know why this matters, but it feels powerful just to observe him as he makes his own ritual.

"We will go to India and see your country, your mother, and I will be there for you through the entire trip. This sword will be a symbol of the rock that I will be for you." He says as he stares deeply into my eyes.

I am now softened to the idea. I have someone who will go with me and support me on my trip.

I am scared to death, but I am curious to see what she looks like and… we could just spend a couple of days with her.

"Okay I will find her through Shirley. She will find out from Rabeya." I speak.

I get Rabeya's address from Mama D and send off a letter telling her I am coming to India.

A couple of months later, an aerogramme arrives with a photo inside. It is a photo of my mother and brother. My first time to see a photo of my brother. It states, "Now you know what we look like. Look for us at the airport."

I can't believe how young she looks and look at my sweet young brother!

I am so excited but also scared to death for December to come. I write journal entries of how it will feel to see her. Imagining it over and over in my head.

The time is here, oh my god I can't believe I am going to India and meeting my mother! I write. This is the last leg of my journey and the last leg of life, as I know it.

It's fast approaching 7a.m.…. Robert and Scott are fast asleep. Scott, my ex, is here to support me also. I am happy he is. I still miss his warm and compassionate ways. I marvel at the way the two of them get along and I feel blessed and supported. Looking out of the airplane window over the horizon, all I can see is what looks like a beautiful sunset, but it is really the sunrise.

After traveling this long through so many time changes, I have no idea what time it is. Amsterdam is far behind me now and so is our layover in Amman, Jordan. Now, we are within minutes of approaching the moment for which I have prepared for so long. My palms sweat, my heart races, and fear swallows me. The flight from Amman is so incredibly different from any other flight I've ever taken. The people are of all origins: Chinese, Dutch, British, and Middle

Eastern. This was a flight that originated in New York City and was headed for Bangkok, Thailand by way of Amsterdam, Amman, Jordan, and Calcutta.

People of all types of religions, languages, and customs are packed onto this one plane. It is unorthodox with people lying on the floor and eating food they brought on board in tin pots. The smells from the food waft through the entire plane as Muslims, Hindus, and Christians are sprawled out with little inhibition. My uptight upbringing surfaces as I look at the strange garb that others wear and the array of head dress that I never see except in National Geographic magazines. The colored turbans of the Sikhs and the middle eastern headdresses that make the men look like Bedouins from the desert are widely varied in color, size, and shape. The women with their rich colored saris, the Muslims with black scarves over their heads, and the European and American women in their gypsy-looking attire or jeans make for a spectacle of a show between airplane meals.

I breathe in deep, close my eyes, and imagine what these next few hours might entail. I have a clear image of my mother in a beautiful sapphire blue sari engulfing my vision. A faint voice speaks a language I don't know. She has her back to me. She is praying. Her long black braid points straight down her back. Her hands are in prayer position. The color of her sapphire sea blue sari is so vivid, wrapping her body in beauty. I can't shake the unique color from my memory. I blink but the same vision appears.

I am losing it from having such a long and tiring trip and I must be hallucinating! Did I take a Xanax without remembering it because of exhaustion? I blink and I see it over and over for the entire flight. It began when we left Amsterdam and is now stopping only a few minutes before we have almost reached Calcutta. It is dark outside but I can't sleep, the vision keeps me awake.

As I look out the window, I feel so close to what created all of us and this beautiful sunrise. We are cruising at 35,000 feet and, at this altitude, I see the world and life differently. I think about the turmoil going on down there with Bosnia and Sarajevo and the chaos, the misery, and suffering everywhere in the world.

Why do we have to live like that when the universe is created in harmony? Hmmm, my life is itself a mirror image of the world but only smaller with internal wars of pain and suffering that I am unable to explain to others.

I hope that flying all this way will bring me some peace of mind and connection to someone like me! A glimpse of similar hands, fingers, toes, eyes, or mannerisms.

The plane begins its descent into one of the most crowded cities in the world, Calcutta, home to Mother Teresa. With a jolt, my mind travels back 25 years to my earliest memories. Dirty streets. Beggars. Hunger.

I remember all the stories about Calcutta. I am prepared for the worst. A horrible, terrible stench filling the air—the stench of cow dung being burned to cook with. I brace myself for the worst possible smell, the most poor, miserable people on the streets, a mother I haven't seen in 25 years and a brother and sister whom I've never seen. As we land, all I think about is my mother and how her arms will feel around me and what it will be like to gaze into her brown eyes. Because of the lack of communication, only through one aerogramme letter, I hope that she really will be at the airport.

Would she know I was coming today, maybe tomorrow? Oh my god, what if she thinks it is tomorrow and I won't know how to find her! I don't have a phone number for her. I hope I told her the right flight number! Oh God what will we do if she is not there? I have no clue how to get around Calcutta! What if India has a different calendar?

We land and the doors are opened to the tarmac. I immediately feel a peace I've never felt before. As we walk down the stairs and onto the ground, I realize there is no smell except maybe some smog and already I am comfortable and feel I am at home, rather than in "India." As we go through immigration and customs, I look around at the airport which is minuscule compared to John F. Kennedy Airport.

This can't be all there is to this airport in a city of eleven million! Where is everyone? There is hardly anyone in the airport.

I realize that everyone waiting for arriving passengers is standing through a set of double doors that open to the outside. There is a cyclone fence outside to keep the throngs of people out of the airport. As I eagerly wait to get through customs, I look out and spot a tiny woman that looks just like the pictures I have of my mother, and I see a boy standing to the side that looks just like the pictures of my brother. The anticipation is enough to drive me over the edge. It's taking over an hour to get through customs but the whole time I can see that tiny woman outside and I am sure she is my mother.

For twenty-five years, I have waited for this moment and here it is staring me in the face. As we walk out, she is within a few feet of me. We don't speak a word. We just walk straight to each other, put our arms around each other, and cry. I feel almost as if I am a child and my whole life since I left her was a blur. Nothing else matters now but being with my own flesh and blood mother. After we stop our embrace, my mother puts a lei around my neck that my sister Champa made out of Champa flowers and roses. My brother does the same. We are all crying and without words.

"Let's go." Says Banta. He waves for us to go towards the parking lot. He is a short, dark man with my mother who seems to have authority.

Robert, Scott, my mother, Champa, my brother Kamal, my mother's spouse, their friends Faisal, Banta, and Bilal all pile into two small vans. Our gigantic "World Traveler" suitcases barely fit but, somehow, we all manage to squeeze in and stare at one another. The Indians are studying our faces and we are looking at each other in amazement that we made it!

"Your mother, she is making breakfast. We go to her house."
Bilal says in his Indian accent.

"Okay," I say hesitantly. I am afraid to eat their food.

As we drive to her house, I feel as if I am right at home and that
I belong here. It is as if I am *finally* home. Living in America since I
was six years old, I hadn't felt at home. Twenty minutes in Calcutta
and my heart already begins to heal. Here I am with my mother
and my new family.

All I can do is keep looking at her. She is such a sight for my
sullen eyes. She sits in the front seat while I sit in the back. She keeps
turning around and looking at me and we don't say a word.

How can she keep on turning around and still drive? It dawns on
me that the steering wheel is on the other side; she is not driving.

We park on a dusty road near a bridge. The buildings look like
a slum. I am scared. We step out of the car to have dozens of eyes
looking at us. I am not sure what to think.

"These people, they think you are a ghost. They not believe your
mother that you come." Bilal says.

We walk through the maze of people as each eye intently watches.
There are children, old people, men, and women. The sewage floats
in the ditches as we step over them to walk to her house.

*I can't believe I am here and that we are going to eat in this god-awful
place. How clean can the food be? I am going to have to get over my fear
of getting sick from the food.*

I look at Robert and Scott and see the fear in their eyes.

"Nothing will make your mama more happy than cooking for us."

I can't believe how he always seems to know what I am thinking
and knows how to calm my fears.

We all go to her home, and she starts to make us Americans
breakfast.

"Mummy make you English breakfast. Eggs and toast." Bilal says.

"Eggs are the one thing that made me sick in the Gulf but we
can't say no." Robert whispers.

She boils water for chai while squatted over a small camp stove on the ground outside her front door. It is a communal outdoor area for all her neighbors as well. She is in charge and orders my sister to do this and do that. Champa is obedient. She is twenty-five years old, under five feet, and has the face of an innocent child. Between demands, they both steal glimpses of me as I sneak peeks of their eyes. Kamal keeps his distance, but I notice his subtle looks at Scott and Robert. He is twenty-one, so skinny, and looks malnourished. He reminds me of Thomas with his thick hair and similar big smile. He is taller like I am. We both got the height. Mummy has the red streaks in her hair just like I get from the sun.

I can't believe I am looking at my blood family that looks like me and, even more so, I can't believe I am sitting here in a slum in Calcutta!

The neighbors don't leave. They stay and watch while giving each other looks and smiles. There are close to thirty people or more watching my every move. As I drink the chai, they smile with satisfaction and give my mother nods. As I eat eggs and toast, they smile more and wait for my reactions.

Robert is right, there is nothing that could make my mother happier right now than us eating her cooking. Her eyes tell everything.

Her home is about eight feet by eight feet with bright blue walls. She has a woven rope cot outside where my brother sleeps. Inside, there is a tiny television, a double bed with her clothes underneath, a ceiling fan, and a refrigerator like the one I had in my dorm room at college.

Bilal explains that they see Mother Teresa walk here almost every day. By American standards, this looks like the poorest of the poor but in Calcutta, this is considered middle class. The people in her neighborhood were like her family. They are all still looking to see if I had really come and if I was real. So many people told her I would never come back but here I was, so everyone had to have a look. The people in this community were stunningly beautiful. The children with their white teeth and large smiles had a beauty about them that

I had never seen in America. They didn't look like the poor kids on the UNICEF commercials.

I could now be proud of the way people from India looked. These were some of the most beautiful children I had ever seen.

They gawk with wonderment and smile. I later learn they did not believe my mother really had a child in America who was coming to visit.

We spend the next couple of nights in a small guest house that cost only eighteen dollars. There are three beds in one big room with a "Western bathroom." The beds are hard, and I am not sure the sheets are even clean. I can't sleep much and am constantly fitful. I cry when I wake up. I spend hours at night thinking about who I was and who I am now. I listen to the Muslim chanting outside to Allah every morning and have no idea what they are saying but it stirs my deepest emotions and I cry continually.

Am I an American or an Indian now? Who is really my family? I don't truly fit in either country. I am not traditionally Indian like my family here and I am the adopted girl at home. I don't really belong here and I don't really belong in America.

After three nights of being awoken by the Muslim chanting at predawn, I found my emotions breaking down uncontrollably more and more. In one way, it was just like the previous mornings when I cried. This morning was different because I couldn't hide my emotions anymore and I couldn't control the crying. I simply lay there crying wondering, "*Who am I?*"

I am not really Indian and I don't fit here in India but then again, I have never felt I belonged in America either.

The torment is so great, I am beside myself in sorrow. I just can't stop the crying.

Just like the last two mornings, this morning Bilal comes with Kamal and they bring a Calcutta Times in English with chai, eggs, and toast already cooked by Mummy. It is kept warm in a stackable tin container and delivered to our room at the guest house. When they come to the door and knock, Robert opens the door and they can see me lying on the bed and that I am crying. They don't say anything, and I pretend that nothing is wrong.

A few hours later, my mother shows up at the door with an entourage of people. I answer the door this time and I cannot believe my eyes—Mummy has the beautiful blue sari on that I saw her in when I had my visions on the plane. Bilal helps Mummy as she talks in broken English.

"I prayed for you to come back for 25 years and today we go to the Kali temple for thanks. God answer my prayer." She says as she points to the heavens.

I've stopped crying so that she will not see me like this. She throws a plastic bag on the bed and pulls out a *salwar kameez* that she bought for me. I feel awkward, not knowing how to wear this everyday outfit in India.

Oh God, I have to wear this for her! I didn't want to wear Indian clothes! I can't say no!

It is a two-piece dress and pants that match with a scarf to drape over the shoulders. I've never worn one of these and feel so foolish, but I have no choice. I must put it on to go with my mother to the temple.

I spent most of my life trying to be American and fit in with jeans and now I have to get out of my box to fit in with my Mummy and India.

She abruptly ushers everyone out of the room and it is only Champa, Mummy, and me. She whisks me into the bathroom and gives me the clothes to put on.

How the hell do these gigantic pants fit? They are big enough to fit a 300-pound woman! Actually, they are damn ingenious because I can just tie them with the drawstring to fit any waist size!

She turns her head towards the corner and gives me respect that I have never known in the home that I grew up in. Shirley always stared at me when I showered and when I changed.

This is so amazing to me that she gives me privacy like this. It means so much to me.

I quickly throw on the clothes, so I don't make her wait. The top goes over my head and the softness of the material and the feel of it next to my body gives me a peace I haven't felt with any clothing I am accustomed to. The outfit is blue with pink flowers and matches the blue in her sari.

I feel so elegant. Wow, do these clothes feel awesome! They're not so constricting! I can breathe!

"OK" I say with a childish giggle.

I feel awkward yet so comfortable in my own skin. She turns around and puts the scarf around my neck. I feel special. Mummy takes care of me. I feel like her daughter now. I feel more myself now than I did with my tight jeans. We hug and I hysterically unleash a cry on her shoulder. She wipes the tears from my cheek.

How can clothing transform how I feel about myself? I will always remember this as a moment that is changing my definition of myself. I do belong here. Here with my Mummy. We come back out into the room and open the door to find everyone rushing back in the room to see me in my new outfit. It seems as if they had their ears pressed on the door listening the whole time. Photos are flashed and I find a piece of me that I never knew was missing in these clothes. This outfit brings me a sense of peace, dignity, respect, love, and connection to my culture and to my mother.

We swiftly take off to squeeze into two small cars and go to the temple to give thanks to Mummy's Kali God for my return.

Returning as the homing pigeon did is an instinctual deep soul need. I, too, had returned home fulfilling one of the most sacred needs of humans. The connection of a mother to a child. The blood coursing through my veins carries the same genetics as the woman who stands next to me. The way she carries herself, the fingers, the eyes, and the bottomless pit of sadness in her eyes links us like a chain. I now root myself into the ancestry of that which could never be taken away from me, my lineage, and my family. We are like the lei of Champa flowers intermingled with roses, all individually unique and beautiful while linked with the string that creates unity to magnify the beauty of an undying and enduring love.

CAMELLIA GINGER
कमीलया अदरक

W AKING UP IS, AT TIMES, A disappointment but I've learned to manage the past through meditation, writing, or making myself simply be positive, but today is different.

The blankets get thrown off, teeth are brushed, and lemon water is gulped. An excitement erupts after the initial disappointment that haunts me most days. A new sense of confidence and wonder comes at the thought that I get to make chai for Bruce, my husband, and for myself! Who the hell thinks *that* can get you out of your funk but for me, that's what it is!

With lighter steps and joy in my feet, I float downstairs. All I can think about is *I get to make the chai I so badly want to drink, and I get to share it with my sweet husband.*

I shake the gallon-sized plastic ziploc bag filled with what my father-in-law calls "dirt" but is actually the golden sunshine I live for each morning. The calling to the deepest part of who I am. The umbilicus to my soul. He only means to make me laugh but does not know the deeper meaning of the journey that I am embarking on with each cup of my homemade chai.

Like a child with glorious anticipation, I grab my magical bag of "dirt" and masala mix. The door of the refrigerator is flung open, and I admire the ginger root awaiting me. With assured confidence I say, "Good morning, Love, do you want a cup of tea?" Bruce's eyes light up as he tells me he would love some. I see his anticipation and feel my heart flutter because he has grown to appreciate the tea as much as I have, though, for different reasons.

This practice of the art of making chai has been in progress for 10 days now. I have transitioned from feeling like a child making mud pies to producing a cup of solid Indian chai that makes my heart sing. It's been a process of trying without forcing and going from enjoying the mediocre cups to learning to trust my instinct and add what is missing to make it perfect. I began 10 days ago by tasting my creation without judgment and have ended up loving the rediscovery of my Indianness.

The small saucepan comes out. There is something different that has happened the last two days. Magically, my intuition and greater guidance now shows me the way to make it properly the first time! Each empowering step feels drenched in grace and transformation. Not only this time but every time. The water pouring into the cup has the power to transform who I am. As soon as the cup is filled, I pour it slowly, watching every drop of goodness go into the saucepan. Soon, this water will serve us as a tool to journey to another land. As I unlock the bag of dirt storing the long-leaf tea and hold it between my fingers, it lives up to its name of "gold." Dirt to one can be gold to another. This is my golden ticket to the me who resides deep within and is dying to be acknowledged.

The clink of silverware as I grab a spoon leads to a subtle quiet dig into my priceless dirt. One, then two spoonfuls to delicately pour into the pure water. As the leaves float, I sense the impending power of heat. The masala is next with just a tad bit tossed in. Reaching for the shredder to add the ginger brings me to the place when I first met the same learning curve.

Skirmishes between Pakistan and India had erupted, and the United States had begun bombing Cambodia. The world lost Malcom X and Winston Churchill in 1965. The Rolling Stones were popular for their song, "I Can't Get No Satisfaction."

My memories swirl and mix with the present-day steam from the cashew milk as I stir...

Poor girl turned chai servant comes to bloom. I don't have shoes. My feet are always dirty on the bottom. I am active. No one watches me at times.

Rabeya calls me upstairs to her apartment, "Come here Bengali girl."

I keep my exasperation private and reply respectfully, "But I am Punjabi."

I don't know English but speak in Bengali to her. I run up the stairs to see what she wants. She is very demanding with her tone, and I am responsive to her authority. I run, trying to skip one stair at a time, but I miss one and fall to my knees.

"Come child, you must hurry."

I jump to attention and fly up the stairs. She ushers me in to her apartment but not without washing my feet in the tub of water by her door. "Your feet must be clean to enter my house."

"Today, you are going to learn to make chai for me," she informs me.

I bounce in with clean feet. I keep looking at them noticing that they really aren't as brown as I thought.

"You are a lovely and very intelligent girl; I would like you to make me chai every day. You can be my chai maker." I am excited. She stands over me and holds my hand as to make the tea with me.

"See you take sprinkles of this tea. Hold it between your fingers as you drop it in so the tea can feel your love and spread it in a circle over the water." I studiously work to make my circle.

"Once you spread the love over the water, add one tiny bit of joy which is the spice mix of masala to the water. The ginger, which keeps me from getting sick from being around all these poor people, is the last ingredient. It is powerful and packed with juice that will heal even the most distraught heart."

Rabeya retrieves the knife and begins to chop the ginger. She instructs me to make sure to put all the juice in with the tea. "The juice is the heart of the tea. I will show you later how to chop the ginger so you can do it all by yourself."

She prays over the tea and tells it to bring her health and a strong body. The leaves, masala, and ginger slowly begin to churn in the kettle. She watches it intently telling me how "it must be done at the right temperature to make the flavor good."

The aroma is captivating, and the intensity of her watchful eye demonstrates patience to me and belief in what can come. Her eyes look at me as if to say she loves me. "You learn how to make chai and you will understand your life," she mutters. "Your eyes shine the truth of your soul, and your soul is deep. Always remember the truth is captured in the soul and shared through your words." I see the sunlight behind her through the window and watch a small bird flutter by.

Every day I come to Rabeya asking to make chai. Day after day we practice, and she tells me how I will someday travel the world like she does. "The world is full of interesting people and beauty that you will one day want to see. You will go to faraway places and make chai for many people. Remember to sprinkle the love in a circle and to not throw it in one place as if it is not important. Carry the joy in every part of life and be the one that can infuse anything with joy."

I STIR MY CHAI ON the stove as my husband waits patiently. I think about how I'm so very grateful for learning this art at such a young age. Weeks of practicing our daily ritual were filled with exciting moments. Rabeya brought me hope, and during those chai-making lessons, I learned about how to live life infused with love.

As I methodically stir, a forgotten memory is surfacing...

I WAKE TO VOICES OF unfamiliar language in the distance. The voices come from a lady and a man. My parents are already gone. They left before the light of dawn. The locks on the door that had always been familiar are no longer there. I have the freedom to run anywhere. I wander and follow the voices which lead me to Rabeya. Our morning ritual of making chai is disturbed by the visitors whose unfamiliar voices boom at her door. As I peer from downstairs in the courtyard, I watch them enter her home. She shuts the door and I begin to feel sad. No chai today. I begin to walk back in our house and the door from Rabeya's opens.

"Bengali girl, come up here!" She hollers. I make my way to the top of the stairs, and she says, "Come, come, I want you to meet my family and make them chai."

I GO BOUNDING UPSTAIRS AND wash my feet hurriedly, forgetting to dry them.

"No, no, no, you must dry them too! You remember God likes a clean house but also, a dry floor," Rabeya quips.

I am excited to meet these people and am not thinking about any rules. I look up from my feet as I wipe the water off. There is a tall dark man and a very white lady. Rabeya puts her hand on my shoulder and says, "This is my brother Mr. Mukerji and his beautiful wife Rose, from America."

Having tunnel vision for my quest, I reply, "Auntie, can I make chai today?"

Rose comments, "My goodness, *you* are making chai?"

"She has been learning. She does everything but cut the ginger," Auntie Rabeya explains.

Rabeya has been in my life since my parents moved to Calcutta. My father was offered a job with her at the tobacco plant, so we moved here shortly after I was born. Every lady who is a friend of my family is my auntie.

"Rose is your new auntie and Mr. Mukherji is your new uncle," Rabeya proclaims.

Eager to show them what I can do, I reply, "Okay Auntie, I am ready to make chai. Can I do the ginger today?"

Rabeya responds happily with, "Today is the day I will show you how to cut and chop to get the ginger just right." We leave the room and move to our usual place near the stove to prepare to make the chai. Dust motes dance in the sunlight streaming through the window as I climb up on my stool.

"Auntie only likes a small amount of ginger. She is not keen on the taste as much as uncle. We will make her cup first," Rabeya explains. She gets the kettle of water and I jump to get the ingredients, which I notice she has moved so I can reach them easily. She knows I want to make it every day.

I hold the tea in my hand and feel the love go from my heart to my hands and reach the tea. I circle it just like Auntie told me to. A pinch of masala for joy and now the ginger. Auntie holds my hand, glides the small knife along the ginger, and begins saying, "This will…" I interject and finish her sentence, "heal and protect us from all the poor people." Rabeya proceeds, "You are not like all the other poor people."

I am inquisitive about poor people and seek clarification. "Who are the poor people, Auntie?"

She fervently explains, "Those dirty people who do not have a clean body, clean clothes, or food. That is why you always wash your feet before coming into my house. I do not want that to enter my house."

Still confused, I ask, "Okay, so I am poor but when I wash my feet, I am rich?"

"Come, let's serve Auntie Rose with your chai."

I find the small cup and saucer. Rabeya pours it into the cup. I carry it to Rose and say, "Special for you, Auntie, and made with love and joy." She smiles and takes the tea to her lips. "Pushpa, I can tell this chai is full of special love and joy."

I say, in all seriousness, "But you might want more ginger to protect you." My new uncle and auntie break out in laughter with Rabeya. "Why do you say that, Pushpa?" I answer with, "Auntie, you said it protects you." I thought they were rich. They were foreigners.

During the last few days of practicing my chai talents, I have learned to recognize when my chai needs a little more love or joy and when it needs a ton more ginger. Chuckling at that memory, I realize now it is only for health benefits and the added flavor rolling around on my tongue.

Perhaps there is another reason. Do I have an embedded residual belief that this will fight the poor and uncleanliness of life? As an adult, I hate shoes in the house and have become a clean fanatic not knowing that this may be where this came from.

Living on a farm in Oregon with my adoptive family, I had a difficult time adjusting to my new life. Muddy dogs and boots coming into our house created dirty floors. Raining outside for nine months of the year created the need for boots and playing in mud puddles most of the year. Mama D did not waste her time cleaning our house. Our cows and horses always had a spotless barn though. Our garden was meticulously taken care of. The house was just a place to sleep and eat. Mama D was not a housekeeper and she let us know that she wasn't.

We used toilet paper which was considered dirty in India. I was disgusted when I had to use it. I didn't like the dust and cobwebs or the dust bunnies on the floor from the dogs. I decided we were poor. Fifty acres in the sticks and a 5-bedroom house did not appear to be anything but poverty to me. In my mind, dirty equated with poverty.

Today, my home, my car, and my body must be clean, or I feel poor. An angst paralyzes me at the thought of anyone coming into my house or getting in my car without cleaning themselves first. Not one day goes by that I don't have anxiety and talk about my home or car being dirty. I don't go barefoot outside and only go barefoot inside if I have just cleaned the floor.

Today as I make chai, I feel it in my fingers: the gold "dirt" and dream of where it must have grown. The tea that comes from India never sees the flowers of the Camellia tea plant bloom. The leaves are picked while they are young before they get a chance to bloom. I, too, have not bloomed. I glance at the package to see the words "Jaago Re," and go to Google translator to find that the meaning is "wake up." I am waking up every day to new memories through smells, taste, and colors. Some memories haunt me and some put jagged edged pieces of scattered memories into seamless insight as to who is behind the brown eyes.

PLUM BLOSSOMS
बेर का फूल

"WHILE STANDING WITH FEET HIP WIDTH apart, halfway lift, back straight, breathe in and then bow forward and breathe out getting that stretch all the way down your spine. Toe heel your feet together, exhale, and come all the way up to Mountain pose. Reach up, spark the hands and feel powerful in this pose. Ground down with your feet, feel your firm foundation," Jack, another yoga instructor, says.

My gaze wanders from the blue sky out the window to the front of the room to see Jack standing in mountain pose with his arms up and smiling. His lat muscles protrude from his mountain and his legs fiercely scream firm foundation with each quad rippling. His muscles are a copy of that on muscle charts from college anatomy and physiology classes.

My freakin' feet are killing me and I feel like I'm rolling around on marbles, but Jack's muscles are enough to keep me still as long as he wants us here! There is always pain and suffering! God, I envy how effortlessly easy he makes yoga look while my body screams for help!

The balls of my feet ache. The feeling of rolling around on marbles while standing in my mountain causes pain and suffering. I envy how effortlessly easy he makes yoga look. When I get a peek of a brightly colored tattoo on his shoulder with beautiful soft red flowers and small Chinese writing in black, I feel a tension in my chest and an unpleasant memory surface. There is an immediate disliking for anything that remotely looks like Chinese art for me. It transforms me to a place, an uncomfortable place within me that I don't want to revisit. "Find your foundation in your feet," Jack utters.

Grasping the floor with my toes and feet, I realize that a firm foundation is as elusive in yoga as it is in life.

How the hell am I supposed to have foundation when I had everything ripped out from under me since I was a small child? It is annoying how people think it is that simple. Come on Jack, can't you tell I am adopted, and I was taken from my mom? Can't you tell I've lived a hard life? I didn't have a perfect life like you did with your mom and dad and culture!

"Reach for new, and root down in your foundation so you can stand powerfully in your mountain."

That stupid Chinese tattoo just has to keep reminding me of how I have no fucking foundation!

I search in my mountain for foundation to no avail. The memories of my college years come flooding back as I feel my throat choking up. Those were the years I truly felt rootless and unable to function. I hold back the tears.

I RECALL LATE FALL OF 1981, just another gray, drizzly day of Sophomore year at Oregon State and the phone rings. I answer with "Hello."

"Hello honey, it is your mother."

"Hi, how are you?"

Mama D says, "Don't you think it is about time you saw Rabeya? She has been here for almost a month, and she hasn't even seen you."

"I don't want to see *that* woman!"

"She came all the way from India to visit and your father and I can't keep making excuses about why you can't come to see her."

I protest in silence.

"How about coming for dinner tomorrow night?"

"No, I can't and honestly, I really don't care about seeing her!"

"But she is the one who helped us to adopt you. She did all the work for us to have you. I really feel indebted to her."

She can feel indebted to her all she wants, what the hell do I owe her?

For the last few weeks, my mother has called me and updated me on their visit. Rabeya had Daddy driving her all over the place at her every whim. He was returning skeins of yarn that were not right and doing every little errand she desired while she was asking who was going to draw her bath for her. She had servants doing such things for her at home in India. Mama D had complained about how high maintenance she was and that she was wearing them out.

"She would love to see how you have turned out, and to know that you are happy and doing well."

Rabeya was the only reminder of the Indian girl I was. I had been just fine the last 13 years making myself into a real American girl and I pushed anything to do with India away from me as far as I could get it.

"She has to see you and know that she did the right thing by sending you here. We will not allow you to keep making excuses anymore. You are putting us in a bind here by avoiding her."

"I really don't want to!" I continue to protest.

"Well, we don't always get to do everything the way we want to in life."

God, I hated it when she said that to me. Life was never the way I wanted it to be and now I felt that it was beginning to go in a direction that made me full of more anxiety.

"We need you to do this. She is making us crazy. Your father will bring her into town and drop her off at the Chinese restaurant for an hour."

"Okay." I concede. "Can we do it tomorrow so I can get it over with?"

"Yes! I am so glad you are going to meet. She is a handful, but I know she means well."

"Alright, alright, I will see you tomorrow."

"Daddy will bring her at noon. I will let him know."

Damn, I can't get out of it now. I am committed to being there tomorrow! Why did she need to see me anyway? She tossed me on a plane to come here years ago and now all of a sudden, I have to be at her beck and call because of some need she has to know that I am here and okay? I fretted through the whole night and the next morning wondering how this meeting that I never, in my craziest imagination thought would happen, was going to go.

I feel hatred for her that is like a burning and raw open wound that someone poured alcohol into. I don't want to have anything to do with my Indian life. For the past 13 years, I've pushed India behind me and walked forward as an American girl. I no longer speak with an Indian/British accent. I know American slang and wear Levi's jeans, go to fraternity parties and football games. I don't want some old lady that knew me as a poor child in Calcutta to mess up my image of being American.

I can't believe that my past is going to be sitting across a table from me. As noon approaches, I become nervous, worried I am going to lose a piece of myself by seeing Rabeya. She was the one who did my adoption, arranged everything, did all of the legal paperwork needed in India, communicated with my adoptive parents and sent me to the airport in a cab to get on a plane to come to America. She had come for this visit to meet my parents for the first time and to see me. They only corresponded for years through letters. Now they finally got to meet in person.

The past years were all about being someone that fit this new life and now I had to see someone that knew me before. It terrified me. No one I knew had ever been to India and no one in my family really knew what my life was before being adopted. I was the girl that knew four languages, that independently ran the streets in tattered, dirty clothes and bare feet, starved, admired her handsome father, played poker with men, watched a man die, looked like everyone else, never thought about fitting in, and who had now become so good at being fake, that this was the real me. I was no longer an Indian but a real American. I was proud of the hard work I had gone through: the constant studying of Americans and metamorphosing myself into the person I thought I could blend into and become part of the fabric of this culture.

Now, I was going to meet this woman. While my boyfriend, Chris, drove the green Toyota Corolla, I rode in the passenger seat fearing for my life. Why? I wasn't sure. I was just scared; my past was coming to slap me in the face, and I had no idea what was ahead of me. *What is it that she wants from meeting me?*

"Are you okay, Puff?" Chris asked. This was the nickname he fondly called me. He was a sweet guy with a generous heart, always there supporting my emotional ups and downs while he worked two jobs and attended college.

I shrugged my shoulders and looked out the window to hide the tears welling up in my eyes. I wore my Levi's 501 jeans and my Oregon State University sweatshirt. We looked like a couple of average college kids. That's all I wanted. I shuddered to think that she may wear a sari. Or, that everyone might think we were relatives. On the drive over, his big blue eyes embedded with red jagged lines looked over with concern and asked, "Are you going to be alright? Do you want me to go with you?"

"No, no, it's okay. I think I have to do this on my own." I lied.

"I am just worried about you. It seems like this will be a tough meeting for you."

"I can do it. It is only an hour and then it will be over."

"I will be there for you when you are finished."

"Yes, I know. Thank you."

"Maybe it won't be as bad as you think."

I could only hope that I was just making this bigger than it really was.

His face was like the full moon: big, bold, and filled with the promise of an expansive life as he smiled and said, "I love you and I will be here for you."

With his strong presence by my side, I know I can get through this. He would be there when I finished lunch to pick me up and I could go on with my day.

Driving into the parking lot of the Riverside Hotel, I notice the attached Chinese restaurant. In front of the restaurant, I see Daddy already parked in his dark blue Nissan King Cab Pickup Truck. There is a tiny woman on the passenger's side just barely big enough to see out the window.

"There is my dad," I point out. Chris slowly pulls into the parking space next to them and all I can see was the small head peering through the window while my dad is obviously explaining to her that it is me in the car next to them. As she climbs out of the truck, my biggest fear is realized.

Great, she is wearing a sari.

As we exchange introductions, I hesitate to hug her. She is a woman of very small stature, short, but a power pack of passion and energy. Her coconut-oiled, shiny, blackish brown hair is parted straight above the center of her nose and pulled back tightly into a single braid falling down her lower back. She wears a soft, flowing sari with threads of brightly colored pinks and gold sprinkled on a sky-blue background. On her forehead, a red dot worn proudly and around both of her tiny wrists are multiple jingly bangles inlaid with sparkly clear diamond-like and colorful false stones.

I don't want people to think we are from the same culture or, even more humiliating, that she may be my mother! I am embarrassed and ashamed of where I once came from and who I was in the past, just a poor girl from the poorest city in the world: Calcutta. I wanted nothing to do with my beginnings.

"I will be back in one hour, Pooh." Daddy says.

"Okay," I say as my voice shakes.

"See you later Puff, I will be back promptly in one hour."

Chris hugs me goodbye and waves at me. That last little feeling of a safe haven drives away.

Thank God I have him to go back to. He is the only thing I can hang onto.

I walk into the restaurant with this sari-clad woman, her bangles jingling and heavy Indian accent exclaiming, "It has been so long since I have seen you, why don't you answer my letters?"

I rush her in and avoid answering her by talking to the hostess.

"Hello," the young girl says.

"Hello," I reply quietly.

"Will there just be the two of you today?" She continues.

"Yes, only the two of us." I answer.

Oh my god, this place is full of people, how embarrassing! We are the only Indians here and I have to be here with this woman in a sari! I hope no one notices!

It's too late; there are not many Indian women let alone women with saris on in this town of only thirty-five thousand. EVERYONE is looking at us. I am frantic. I need to sit down and hide out in a booth.

"Could we please have a booth?" I beg. Anything so that I can disappear and not be seen.

The hostess shuffles us back to the booth and we sit while she hands us the menus. Above us, a cheaply framed print of plum blossoms with Chinese writing in black stands out from the wall.

That picture reminds me of that ancient Chinese proverb I love: "A bit of fragrance clings to the hand that gives flowers." I heard that quote somewhere and loved it! For all I know, this writing could say anything.

Rabeya takes her sweater off. I look at the menu. Then, the interrogation begins.

"Pushpa, why you not wearing Indian clothing?"

I look at her with disbelief. *Is she really asking me this? Did I just hear what I think I heard???* Anger is bubbling. *How dare she, how can she expect me to be anything Indian after sending me here, where in the world does she think I am living?*

"What is wrong with my clothes, I am an American now you know?" *How the hell does she expect me to wear Indian clothes when I have not even had anything other than American clothing for 13 years? Where am I going to buy a sari for God's sake?*

Since I was adopted, I have not seen many Indian people. I have not eaten Indian food. I have not worn Indian clothes. *I am American! It is so uncool to be wearing a sari!* I swallow my anger. Now it is boiling in my stomach!

"Okay, so are you ready to order?"

The waitress comes. "Can I get you something to drink?" She asks pleasantly.

"We are ready to order, I am sort of in a hurry," I reply.

Rabeya looks at me like she doesn't know what I am talking about, she has barely sat down and seen the menu.

I need to eat and get out of here before I blow up in public!

We order and the waitress looks at me, noticing I am uncomfortable.

"I will let them know that you are in a hurry." She says to me.

"Thank you," I breathe. *I think this girl must know that I am pissed off! I can hear my heart pounding! I gotta control myself!*

Again, it is just us looking at each other across the table. I am sort of intrigued with looking at her face close up and seeing some of myself. It distracts me from my anger. *Does she look like me? She is Indian, we must look alike. Do I look like her? We both have the same skin coloring, and her eyes are brown and shaped like mine.*

This is my first time looking at another Indian face so closely. I am examining her in detail. *I wonder if she looks at all like my mother. She probably does. She is an Indian woman. No, I think my mother was* much uglier. *My mother must look poor and old by now. Rabeya looks young and attractive.*

"Was that your boyfriend that drove the car?" Rabeya asks.

"Yes, that was my boyfriend. We have been dating for about six months now." I answer back. *Finally, she is talking to me about my life!*

"Why are you dating an American boy, why not an Indian boy? You should be dating an Indian boy," she spews at me.

That is it! I can't take this freak telling me how I should be living my life! How the hell am I supposed to meet an Indian boy? I think Indian boys are ugly! I am fuming inwardly while ignoring her questions.

"Is our food almost ready?" I beg the waitress as she walks by.

I am afraid of my own anger. It is almost uncontrollable. My face feels like it is about to explode!

"I will check, it should be here shortly," she says, clearly annoyed.

Do I have to defend who I am? The person I have worked so hard to become and my country that I am so proud to be a citizen of? What is wrong with who I am? God, what the hell was I thinking coming to this public place with such a moron? This woman is nothing but an uppity bitch that thinks she can just roll into my life and tell me what to do. Who the hell does she think she is? She is ruining me!

The food comes. I eat a few bites while my stomach churns and aches. I can't eat anymore. Few words are spoken as I gulp bites of shrimp fried rice. I watch the clock and eagerly wait for Chris. *Please come save me Chris!!!*

I see a flash of green in the parking lot, I swiftly head for the door. I have nothing to say to her, nothing in common with her. *I am done with this witch!*

WEEKS LATER

This one incident takes me over the edge. I am really lost as to what my identity is now.

Who am I? Who am I supposed to date? Am I a fake? Am I living a lie? Is Rabeya just a judgmental asshole who knew nothing about being American?

I am miserable even though I have a beautiful one-bedroom apartment in one of the nicest complexes in the city. I am living the college life of a kid who "has money," not the norm of sharing an apartment with 3-4 others. It is a nicely decorated place with large potted plants and all new wicker furniture with brown and rust colored tropical leaf designs on the pillows. Mama D buys me the furniture with the stipulation of giving it back to her after school. She always has rules applied to anything she gives me.

I have been living here for several months and am desperately lonely being all by myself. I really have no friends at this college since I never lived in a dorm here and spend most of my time working at Arctic Circle giving out burgers and fries, running, playing tennis, doing aerobics classes, going on long bike rides, or spending time with Chris.

A beautiful apartment, a great boyfriend, and free time to do whatever I want. It still doesn't fill the emptiness in my heart. In the crevasses of my brain, I just fixate on not knowing who I am.

What had I done wrong to become so different from what she thought I should be? Should I have kept all my culture and not tried so hard to meld into my environment? I can't stop feeling as though I have let Rabeya down. Would my real parents be just as disappointed in me?

The last few months, I've exercised like I am training for some special event. Anytime that I am not at school, studying, or working, I am a machine working out. It serves as a much needed mental release.

My kitchen has bare cupboards, no food but some butter and bread in the fridge. It's not because I don't have money for food. My parents give me money for everything as long as I am going to school. I am also working part-time at a restaurant, so I never have to do without any material things that many college students are scraping by to have such as food or rent. From the outside, I have a great life and it appears as though I have it all together. People think I am pretty, smart, and have everything going for me. College boys are asking me out on the way to class, after working out at the gym, and they even follow me home to find out where I live so they can knock on my door and ask me out.

I still think I am unwanted, unattractive, and that I stick out like a sore thumb.

There are no girls I connect with, only girls that are party friends. Thus, I spend most of my time alone and working out to keep myself sane.

I wish I could have one true friend, one that I can talk to about my deepest, darkest pain. That damn so-called best friend from high school just dumped me in a seven-page letter! She thinks she is too good for me. I am not "cultured enough." She is probably right.

Today is just another day, class in the morning and then I race home to get my running shoes on so I can jog between rain showers to the recreation center to take an aerobics class, jog back, and then ride my bike for 10 miles.

Between class and exercise, I bring out the one thing that is a loyal friend to me. It is always there to lift me up and to help me feel great about myself. *I always have my cocaine! I love it. It makes me feel invincible! I am a badass with this shit!*

I open the cupboard and slide out a piece of glass I took out of a beautiful picture frame. It now stays in the cabinet with a razor blade and little mountains of cocaine.

The cocaine makes me feel like anything is possible and that I am not some fragile and delicate poor, tiny Indian girl but a strong American girl who can endure even the toughest of workouts and conquer the deepest of pain.

The cocaine helps me feel full of life and keeps me so hyper that I can go all day long from one physically taxing thing to another. *I don't have to feel like a freak anymore! I don't have to be depressed! I can shove that emotional shit away! I don't even need food!*

The routine is always the same: race home a mile from class with a backpack loaded with books and a tennis racket. A large umbrella keeps the mist of the day off me. I shake it vigorously as I come in and drop it just inside the door.

My heart races as I get excited just thinking about the lines of cocaine that I know I will inhale. I drop my books then quickly change into my track shorts and t-shirt.

I can't wait to snort a line!

Before even finishing tying my shoes, I jump up from the edge of the bed and run into the kitchen, pull out my glass with the perfectly straight white lines of powder that I prepare every morning. The Bic pen with the inside taken out is the perfect thing to put in the end of my nose to inhale the two lines that have been waiting for me. As the powder disappears with my deep inhalations, I feel the familiar surge of power.

No one can stop me now and no one is better than me anymore. In fact, I am better than everyone else!

Today is different though. On the jog back, I begin to feel weak, reliving my pain as an adoptee in my mind. I am angry, and almost crying from the depth of sadness that is coming to a head in my heart. *If only I could just get rid of this overwhelming pain! I hate feeling this heavy.*

I hold it in a couple more blocks until I get back and run in the door. I sit down at the kitchen table and smash my forehead on it. I am losing it. The sobbing is uncontrollable. It is coming from the abyss in my soul. Everything is getting dark. The realization comes.

I am a nobody, a nothing that doesn't matter in this world. I spend most of my time alone.

Who really, truly cares about me? My only connection to anyone is Chris and he is just a boyfriend. It would be such a relief to not be here anymore, not be living anymore, no one would notice if I wasn't, and the loneliness and pain would all be gone if I just didn't have to have this life anymore. Life sucks! Who needs it?

I look up to see a pair of small, light orange handled scissors sitting in front of me. Everything else fades. *I have heard that if you cut the veins in your wrist, you can die. If only I could have the courage to just do it, I could end this pain in my heart.*

I hold the scissors at my wrist, but I don't have the courage to complete the task.

I am such a wimp! The cocaine makes me feel like I can do anything so why not do another line of that and get my confidence and courage up?

Again, I pull out the piece of glass with prepared lines, grab the pen and deeply inhale to get all I can as quickly as possible into my nasal passages. *Now, I can do this. No one will ever know or care that I am gone. I can do this!*

I grab the scissors and sit down at my kitchen table. Holding the scissors to my wrist slowly rubbing them back and forth and studying my veins. *How do I do it? Fast or slow?*

Everything is disappearing into a void.

I can already feel the pain slipping from my existence. *I no longer have to be this oddity in life or a person that not even my mother loved.*

Deep breaths fill my lungs as I focus on the scissors and how they can just change my life in an instant.

If only I could just rub the scissors harder and cut that vein. I am so close! All I have to do is push them down harder. Sawing at my wrist is not working so I might have to slice it.

A knock comes at the door and Chris bounds through the door with his usual powerful presence and big smile. His face changes quickly.

"What are you doing, Puff?" He sees me sitting at the table with scissors in hand.

"No one will notice if I am gone, I just want to die," I reply matter-of-factly.

"We need to get you some help," he demands.

"No, I don't need any goddamn help!" I say adamantly.

He grabs the scissors out of my hand and throws them down. He forcefully grabs my arm and pulls me up. "I am taking you to see someone!" he bursts out.

I am crying. Through my tears I see a man that is determined. He pulls me out of my apartment, slams the door behind us and throws me in his car. He pulls the seat belt around me. My nose runs as I continue sobbing.

Damn it, Chris, I can't take it anymore. I want to die. I will kill myself! "You should have just let me do it, no one would have cared or noticed!" I scream.

The next thing I know Chris is pulling me by the arm into the college hospital and I am deeply sobbing while yelling at the nurses.

"She was trying to kill herself with scissors!" Chris yells to the nurse.

"I am not crazy, and I don't want to be in a rubber room!" I yell with spit flying from my mouth.

"We want her to spend the night here tonight," the nurse says to Chris.

"No, I am not sleeping here in some rubber room," I argue. "I am not some crazy lunatic!" *These fucking people are conspiring to put me into some room with a straight jacket!*

"She can go home if you stay with her all night and make sure that she is okay," the nurse says to Chris.

"I really don't need him staying with me, I am fine!" I say with a glare at the nurse.

"That is the only way we will allow you to go home tonight." The nurse says with authority.

"Puff, I can spend the night. I will sleep on the floor and if you need anything, I will be right there for you."

I see his eyes and realize that I am hurting him. "Okay, I just want to sleep. I am so exhausted."

"Sign this paper here. It states that you will see a counselor tomorrow at 10:00 in the morning here on campus. I will give you a paper with the information on it and Chris can take you," the nurse says.

"Okay, if that is the only way I can get out of this stupid hospital," I agree.

All night, Chris sleeps next to my bed on the carpet while I sleep fitfully.

The next day, he drives me to the counseling appointment. My body is limp and lifeless, not the sure, strong, confident runner and workout fanatic.

He stays outside as I meet my counselor. "I will be here for you when you get out."

I had counseling in the eighth grade once, so I think I know what to expect. The doctor, a short man with dark hair and upright posture, comes to the waiting room and ushers me into his office. We sit down.

"Tell me about yourself and your life."

"I was born in India and adopted at the age of six."

"Why were you adopted?"

"My mother didn't want me. We were very poor, and they didn't have enough money to take care of me."

I begin crying but never stop talking for 45 minutes. He barely utters a word, mostly listens. I look up at the clock to see the time and we only have five minutes left. Time flew. I feel relief.

"You were adopted at six from India, you are not close to your family, and you feel very lonely and think that you don't matter. You don't know what it is like to see someone who looks like you or has the same blood."

"Yes! Yes!" I proclaim.

"You have no foundation and now you must realize you are the only one who can build a foundation. You cannot build a life without a foundation."

Oh my god, I can't believe it! Someone understands me. An absolute stranger, but he gets me! How in the hell am I going to do this? I know I am the only one responsible for creating this in my life and I am determined to do it some way.

Something so basic yet so profound. It sounds easy in one sense but where was I going to start? I come out of my session awakening to what I am up against in my life and that it is going to be my job and my responsibility to create a foundation for myself. No one is going to give a foundation to me on a platter.

I can't receive it from the people who try to give it to me: my new family. That just doesn't come naturally.

RABEYA DIES YEARS LATER WITH the fragrance of flowers in her hand from all the money she received through my adoption but with leprosy as her ultimate demise. I continue living as the rootless flower growing in a vase while creating roots of my own, a new foundation, my mountain. On my own.

Plucked Flower Blossoms

फूल फूल

M Y FLIP FLOPS DROP ON THE shoe stand while I reach to open the door. A big rush of hot, humid air blankets my already perspiring body while the booming voices of the other yogis flood my ears.

The space I land on is between a familiar faced, late forty-something woman to my left and a thirty-something man who is chiseled to perfection on my right. He smiles and she smiles.

"Hello," I say with a boomerang smile.

I quickly place my tomato red mat between the two of them and cover it with the sunny yellow non-slip cover and run through the maze of other mats to the corner to grab a sky-blue colored block that helps with stretching poses. I am now back in place and set up. Lying back on the mat, I take this time to mentally prepare for class by relaxing and practicing breathing but the roar of voices keeps coming like a wave. Like waves on the rocky Oregon coast, the ebb and flow of voices surround me—getting louder into a crescendo before they quiet into silence and rise again. The rock music of Coldplay is reverberating amongst the conversations.

I like this song, but this feels more like a party than a yoga class. So much for Eastern Yoga, this is definitely the American version.

The voices slowly silence as Matt enters the room and turns the music off.

"Hi everyone."

"Hello Matt!" bursts out a few voices.

They all sound so damn cheery. Can't they just be real and not act so friggin' fake? These people act like this guy walks on water. I don't know, I swear this is like a cult at times!

Matt is short, standing approximately five feet six inches and today he is sporting a tight black tank top and black fitted shorts. Matt is fit, late 30s or 40s, light skinned with black hair. He is the owner of the studio and gets immediate respect from the yoga students. Matt is comfortable in his skin and in his role as an instructor. The rock star microphone over his head gives him an air of authority. He smiles as he walks between the tiny spaces between the wall-to-wall yogis, being careful to not step on a mat or knock over a bottle of water. He clasps his hands.

"Well, let's get to know each other really well and move in closer together to fit more people in the room." He says with his lips so tight.

I feel claustrophobic. There is no sacred space. My heart races as I have to crowd in even closer to strangers.

Why the hell do we pay one hundred dollars a month to be squeezed in like sardines so that they can make even more money? I feel like a number. Just another body. Just another dollar sign.

After we all shuffle and move even closer together, the room seems even hotter. The temperature is set at 87 degrees but with all these bodies confined in this small space, it is sucking the air right out of here.

We haven't even started and I'm ready to pass out. Why did I come today? I knew this class would be packed! I swear I love to torture myself! Too late now to change my mind! I'm stuck.

"Okay, now we are ready to go," Matt says.

"Well, let's start with child's pose. Come onto your knees and bring your toes together at the end of your mat. Start with your knees wide open and bow forward. Sit your butt back down onto your heels. Begin to start breathing in through your nose while your hands reach in front of you. Take this time to be here, come to your mat and be present to yourself and breathe. A deep breath in and a deep breath out, it is that simple. Life is that simple. Always come back to this. Breathe in and breathe out. When things get tough, know that you always have your breath."

"Yoga is meant to be fun." Matt chuckles. "It is meant to be childlike. Breathe in through the mouth; press the forehead into the mat. Bring a childlike quality into your yoga." He continues with his quirky accent.

My lips quiver as I do everything I can to hold in the words that are screaming in my head. *Childlike? What the hell is that? I never had a childhood!*

My eyes are closed as I bow forward.

"Come into this pose as you came into this world without all the stuff filling your head but with the freshness of new life," Matt utters.

A sense of doom comes over me as I continue to breathe. In my mind's eye, flashes of how I came here begin to flood my eyes like on a giant movie screen. The memories that my Mummy shared with me about the beginnings of my life play in my mind.

TAJ PUR INDIA, 1962

"Why don't you just be happy about this child?" My mother begs.

"I don't want a child, not your child," Thomas yells. "You are too black; I don't want a black child." Thomas continues.

"How can you not love this baby already; it is a gift from God!" Shanti cries.

"I cannot love something I do not want." He continues.

"Oh Thomas, God is telling me that you will find a way to love and take care of this child." Shanti fitfully begs.

In a fit of rage Thomas punches Shanti in the belly.

"Stop trying to make it go away by hitting it. It is not going away. You are only hurting our little baby inside me. It is going to be here soon, and it is your child to enjoy!" She screams.

Thomas smacks Shanti across the face and says, "I don't want it!"

Two years later

I am in a dark, small room with no windows. There is one light bulb hanging from the ceiling. It barely lights the room with a shade of dark yellow. I am enclosed in here. There is no way out. The door was locked when Mummy and Papa went out. I heard the sound of the lock after they closed the door. They were arguing with each other as they went out the door and forgot to say goodbye to me. I am sad.

Sitting on the dirt floor with a piece of cloth around my bottom, I feel the dirt and grit of the floor. My hand has dirt on it. I cry for a moment but I know that I am alone so no one will hear me. Crying is futile. I stop the fussing.

I am afraid to move because Mummy and Papa told me to sit still and stay until they come back. My stomach hurts and my mouth is dry. I am so lonely and sad. I close my eyes and want to sleep so that when I wake my mummy will be back. I cannot sleep. I don't know if it is day or night.

I hear the noise of people talking outside. My heart pounds but then the voices fade away. They are gone. It wasn't Mummy and Papa. It was someone else.

I close my eyes again waiting to dream. The dream doesn't come. Only the waiting with my eyes closed. My mouth gets drier. My belly hurts more. I must keep closing my eyes to ignore the pain. My visions come of another day of Mummy carrying me and seeing the sky above me. I feel the warmth of her holding me with my legs wrapped around her waist. She is smiling with her beautiful brown eyes looking at me. I am happy.

My eyes open as I hear the noises again outside. The dream fades. The voices are getting louder and louder. They are at the door. It is Mummy and Papa. They are yelling again. I listen. I am sad. My heart is heavy. My mummy is talking to my papa but she is also crying. I begin to cry. My mummy is crying. I am crying. I am sad.

The clanking of the door being unlocked is loud. It opens with a loud bang against the wall. My papa walks in and smiles at me with his big white teeth. He scoops me up off the floor and cradles me in his arms. He likes me. I think he likes me. He brings his face right up to mine. His breath smells. It is icky and smelly. Mummy is still yelling at him. They are yelling about me. Mummy says my name and cries. They are fighting about me. She is yelling at him.

Mummy hits his arm. He keeps smiling.

"Put my baby down." She shrieks.

He just keeps smiling at me. His eyes are big. He won't stop looking at me.

I love him. He is my papa. He is handsome. He is warm. He smiles at me a lot.

Mummy keeps yelling at him. *Why is she yelling and angry with him? He loves me.*

He is still smiling and looking at me. His eyes are big. He does not blink. I am loved and cradled in his arms.

My back hits something hard. I am way up here high above the dirty floor. The only time I get off that floor. Papa lays me down. I want his arms around me but his arms are gone now. He takes my clothes off my bottom. Mummy is yelling. Mummy is crying. She is grabbing Papa. She is sad. Papa stops looking at my face. He is looking down there where the cloth was on me. He kisses me there. I feel warmth from his mouth. Mummy is crying. His tongue licks me. Mummy keeps hitting him on the back. He ignores her. Then, one arm goes back and hits her. She falls backwards and cries.

"Please God, forgive him for what he is doing. Help me to stop this!" She is crying and praying.

I am floating above looking down.

I see this handsome man with thick shiny black hair with his mouth on my private parts. His nose is rubbing on me. Air is blowing on my skin from his nose. I feel this sensation. As I watch from above, he sticks his finger inside me and kisses me at the same time. It hurts. His fingernails scratch me inside. His teeth bite my body. His eyes are closed now. When will they open again? They stay closed. His breathing gets faster. Mummy leaves. She is sobbing. She closes the door behind her. She gave up.

Looking down past my belly, I see my papa. He doesn't see me. His eyes are closed. It hurts. I see blood on his fingers. I see blood on his mouth and face. I look down from above now. I am floating again.

This is me I am looking at and that is my papa? He loves me.

He starts to take his bloody hand to his pants. He changes hands. His mouth is still on my private parts. I feel the lips there again. They have not moved away. I am looking down past my belly again. I am not floating. He sticks his finger back in. It scratches and hurts again. His lips are tightly on me. His other hand is on his pants. I hear voices. They are outside. I hear a jingling noise. It is the neighbor. That jingling noise is the sound of the neighbor coming home. I miss Mummy. I feel sad.

"Mummy" I cry.

Mummy is not there. I am back up floating above it all.

Papa is grabbing his pants. His hand is in his pants. He is breathing loud. His eyes are closed still. He bites me one last time. He is finished. I am floating above.

He leaves me there.

He wipes his hands. He wipes his face. He changes his pants.

He places me on the dirty floor. I am small. I look at myself from above. My cloth is still hanging around some of my bottom.

I sit. He smiles. I feel my body again. I am not floating.

I am here. I sit. The same place where he picked me up.

He is handsome. He is smiling. He is talking to me. His eyes are open. His hair is black and shiny. He is happy. He touches my face.

"Bye-bye," he says.

I say nothing. I sit. I float.

He opens the door. Some light comes in. It is sunny like in my dream of Mummy and me. He closes the door. Only the yellow light bulb again.

There is chatting outside with a lady. It is not Mummy. He is so happy. He is so sweet to her. *He never talks to Mummy like that.*

They are laughing.

It is quiet. The voices are gone. I am alone just me again sitting on the floor. I look up. That is the place. The place Papa puts me.

ONE YEAR LATER

I am walking with Papa. He holds my hand. I look up. He is so tall. We are walking next door. Papa's job is there. Our apartment is by his job. I am so clean and pretty. I have a new frock on. I have new shoes, shiny, black, new shoes. I am so proud.

My papa is handsome. He smiles at the people when we walk by. He has a pretty smile. He smiles bigger at the ladies, especially the rich neighbor lady that he knows. She is pretty. She wears a sheer purple sari. She smiles a lot. She is nice to me. She tells me to come to her house and get sweets every day.

"You know, Thomas (my papa), she is looking very smart today in her new clothes for school." My papa's friend Rabeya says.

I am happy. My blue dress is so stiff that the collar is standing up nicely.

"The dress is big, but she will grow into it." Rabeya continues.

"Yes, she will be a big doctor one day." Thomas replies.

They both laugh and look at each other.

"This girl will one day bring lots of money and lots of luck to you. She is so pretty and so smart." Rabeya comments.

"You are lucky to have such a handsome and kind father." She says to me. I nod in agreement.

They talk about me going to school.

"You are getting so big; it is time to start going to school," says Rabeya.

I smile at her.

"You have a beautiful smile just like your papa," she says.

They look at each other grinning.

"You can call me Auntie," she says.

"Okay, Auntie," I say politely.

She really likes me and she really likes Papa.

"You come upstairs to my house today and get some sweets, okay?" she continues.

I look at Papa.

"Okay." Papa says and looks at me with a head nod.

"We must go. We will come to your house later," Papa says.

"Bye-bye Auntie."

"Bye-bye."

We leave hand in hand. Walking down the sidewalk, my papa is friendly to everyone he sees. He says hello to strangers. People like my papa.

We walk to the gate to Papa's work. I feel special. The guard looks down from the guard tower, nods his head at my papa as he moves his hand to let us know to come in. Papa knows the guard. They talk and I don't know what they are talking about. I hold Papa's hand tight, my fingers slip from his and I go to grab his hand again. He is in a white shirt and white pants. These are the clothes that he always wears to work.

As I look up, his white clothes fade into the white building behind him. All I see is his eyes and hair.

"Hello Thomas," people say as we walk by. One very tall man stops, bends over, and rubs me under my chin.

"Is this young girl the daughter God gave you that you always speak of?" The stranger says.

"Yes, this is Pushpa, my daughter." He says proudly.

He likes that I am his daughter. I feel so proud.

"She is as lovely as a little flower blossom, just as her name means!" The stranger says.

I must be pretty like a flower!

This is the first time I come to his work. I am so proud to be dressed in my new frock and new shoes, going to Papa's work and holding my papa's hand.

This is a very nice place. I feel so small next to him.

We walk together up the stairs to the guard tower. Everything here is so clean behind that gate.

We enter the guard tower.

"This is my daughter; she is coming to stay at work with me today." He boasts.

"Yes, she is looking so very smart in her frock, and I've seen her walk by the gate before. I know she is your daughter." The guard replies.

I like it up here. I can see so far away.

"I can see the top of that man's head, Papa. There is our house over there and the market over there." I eagerly show Papa.

I like looking at the street and sidewalk. I am so far away from everything down there. This is fun to be high above everyone and everything.

"Papa, I like it up here. This is so fun!" I say excitedly.

The old man here seems good. He brings me sweets and candies. I don't know which one to take from his hands.

"No problem, eat both." The guard says.

He is very skinny, and his clothes are kind of old and dirty. He has icky teeth. One tooth in the front is broken.

I wish he would not smile so I don't have to see his icky, broken tooth.

I look to Papa to see if it is okay. He nods his head to go ahead.

This is fun. I have candies and sweets. I sit down on the chair near the window. My feet have trouble reaching the floor. I enjoy my sweets while Papa talks with the man. He brings out a cigarette and lights it and then gives it to my papa. This is the first time I see Papa smoke. The room gets smelly and smoky. I feel icky. I don't like that smell. I want to leave now. "Can we go now Papa?"

"No, you can stay here while I go to work." Papa says.

"I'm scared. I don't want to stay here."

"Too bad, you will have to while I work. I cannot take you where I am going while I am working today, maybe next time you can come with me."

I am scared to be alone with this man. I don't like that smoke he is blowing out of his mouth.

Papa is ready to go. He bends over, grabs my arms tightly.

"You be nice girl for Papa." He speaks.

My heart pounds, this man now looks scary.

I liked him when he gave me candy, but I am scared to be alone. I wish Papa wouldn't leave me!

He opens the door to leave as my heart beats faster.

"I will be back at lunch time." Papa says.

The door closes behind him. He waves through the window of the door at me. I watch him go down the stairs to leave. I want to cry. My heart sinks. He turns around and waves from the bottom of the stairs.

Maybe he will come back!

I look for him to turn around and come back. He doesn't. He turns around and waves before he disappears in the building. The door closes behind him. He is gone. I am alone with this man. I am scared.

"Do you want another sweet?" He asks.

"No," I answer while I hold my tears.

I sit and wait for Papa. I gaze out the window. No one comes. I tire of waiting and fall asleep. The clamor of people talking and walking in the tower startles and awakens me.

It is break time. Where is Papa?

"Whose baby is this?" A man says as he looks at me.

"This is Thomas' daughter." The guard says.

"Oh yes, she looks very much like him."

The men keep coming. There is lots of cigarette smoke. It fills up the room.

"Are we playing poker today?" One worker says.

"Yes, at lunch," replies the guard.

"I am going to win back some money today, if you stop cheating." The worker jests.

"I did not cheat, you bastard!" The guard retorts.

These men say icky words. Words that I know are bad.

I just want Papa to come but he doesn't.

Finally, everyone leaves again.

The old guard goes out the door and down the stairs. I try to sleep in the chair.

Some sleep hits me but then I awake again. I am confused and sleepy. I look out the window and see Papa!

He is coming back!

He goes in another door of another building. I want to cry as tears come to my eyes. I am lonely here in this smelly place. I am bored. I look around in the room. I walk behind the desk and look down on the floor to see piles of pictures of women, some naked and some with clothes on. There are packs of cigarettes, cards, and little round plastic things. It is as dirty as the guard man that sits behind the desk.

I hear voices. I run back to my chair. I look out the window. There he is with some other men. They are all coming up the stairs. I sit like I never looked behind the desk. I act like I have been sitting in this chair the whole time. They walk in the door and talk very seriously amongst them.

"This man he is very, very big man." One man says.

"We have to get ready for his arrival." Another one says.

They are talking fast.

"Tomorrow will be a very big day. He comes in the morning from America." The guard says.

I am listening but looking out the window.

When is Papa going to come get me? I have to pee. I can't hold it anymore.

The warm trickle rushes out and I pee in my underwear. My frock feels wet under my bottom and feels icky as I sit.

I wish that Papa would hurry and come and get me.

Mummy walks by the gate on the sidewalk on the other side. I stand up straight looking out the window hoping she might see me so I can wave to her and then she will come and get me out of here, but she goes to our house next door.

Where is Mummy coming from? She looks like a Princess. I want to look just like Mummy when I am big.

Mummy is always working for Rabeya, my new auntie that lives above us. She is going places to do things for her. Mummy is always tired from working. She never smiles. I go to the other window while the men keep talking about the "big man from America." I look to see if I can see her go to our house. She disappears behind the building. I am not high up enough to see her anymore. I wish she saw me. My dress is sticking to my bottom.

"Why did you pee? Why did you not ask to go to the bathroom?" The men laugh at me.

I begin to cry. The guard is mad at me.

"Why did you do this? You made a mess for me to clean, and I have enough to do to have this place looking good by tomorrow!" The guard yells.

I cry and feel sad that I made this mess.

The door comes open and there he is, Papa. His big sunny smile saves me.

"She has made a mess all over this chair and office for me to clean up and tomorrow Mr. Brown is coming. He is a very big, big man from America," yells the guard.

"Don't worry I will clean it up," Papa says. He squats down on the floor and begins to wipe my chair with an old towel.

"I have met Mr. Brown and he is a very kind man." Thomas says.

"He is from America, so he is very rich, and we have to have this place perfect for him," yells the guard again.

"Yes, we must have it looking perfect, but he will be so busy that you will only see him come in and go out the gate. I will try to please him with my service that I bring while he eats and talks with the other dignitaries. They are all rich foreigners who love coming to India." Thomas boasts.

"How do you know this, Thomas?" The guard inquires.

He stops wiping the chair. "You have not been working here long but I have been here many years and have experience with these people. They have asked me to serve them many times when they come." Thomas continues.

I am excited.

Papa knows these important people who are coming here from America. I am proud of him. I smile at Papa.

"Mummy is home, can we go home now? I saw her walk there," as I point out the window to Russell Street.

"My God, you did get your frock wet. Next time I bring you, you must ask to go to the bathroom. You cannot do this again." Papa says abruptly. "This man cannot have you doing this in his office." Papa says as he points at the guard.

He grabs my hand as I look up to see his face. He is not angry. He walks me towards the door. *Yaaayyy! We are leaving!*

"Namaskar, my friend, don't worry about tomorrow. There will be no problems and I will not be bringing my daughter with me; she can stay home." Papa says to the guard. I am so happy.

I don't have to come here to this smoky, smelly place tomorrow!

The guard hands me a couple candies as I walk out the door hand in hand with Papa. "Namaskar, thank you," I shyly reply to his warm gesture.

THE FOLLOWING MONTHS

Papa keeps bringing me back to his work. The guard likes me. He gives me candy when we come.

"Thomas, you have a beautiful daughter." He says to my papa.

"Goodbye." Papa says and goes down the stairs.

A smile comes over the guard's face. He talks to me.

"You are beautiful, just like your name means. Beautiful like a flower blossom." He speaks.

He grabs his pants and laughs. He runs at me to tickle me. I run from him. He chases me around the room and then unzips his pants and pulls out his penis. It is wrinkly. He laughs as he chases me. When he catches me, he sticks his penis in my mouth.

Months go by as I spend time listening to men talk during poker games in a smoke-filled room and get chased with his wrinkly penis.

THE NEXT YEAR

At the age of four, I wear my neatly pressed uniforms for school along with my black shiny shoes. I can't stop looking at them and they make me feel important.

The infamous and prestigious Catholic Loreto Boarding School becomes my home. With the funds of Auntie Rabeya, I am given a "proper education." Behind a gate stands buildings dating back to the late 1800s. The grounds are beautiful with large leafy trees bowing over the spacious lawn giving the sense of peace and serenity. The drive sways with haunting shadows of ghosts of past students. To the left, a small chapel graces the landscape for student prayers. In the back are buildings with classrooms and a large cafeteria lined with tables and silverware perfectly placed in waiting for mealtimes.

One of the buildings contains the sleeping porches for the girls on the downstairs and upstairs floors. The older children are downstairs and the younger ones, like me, are upstairs. It is a large expansive room with numerous beds made of a metal mesh with a mattress on top. Large windows embrace the light streaming into the sleeping porch.

We march to class, to meals, and to the chapel. Always in perfectly pressed, white-collared uniform dresses. I enjoy having shiny shoes and a clean dress that I am happy to wear. I like marching to and fro.

I dump my Punjabi, Bengali, and Hindi for English. I must be a proper girl and speak only English unless I want to get hit with a ruler by the nun. Food is now a part of everyday rituals. I like to learn. The girls here are my friends. Many of them have English names. I still wait every day to see my mummy and papa.

DECEMBER 1968

Late in the darkness of night, a taxi picks me up from Russell Street and sweeps me to the airport. Alone in the back seat with a driver, I see the glimpses of Calcutta for the last time. Not knowing where I am going, I meet a woman at the airport who takes me into the building through to my gate to fly away in the big airplane that awaits.

THE FIRST SIX YEARS OF abuse, starvation, poverty, loss of family, loss of identity, loss of culture, speckled the canvas of my life. Feeling as a commodity, I held my value in those things that others valued. The intelligence, cuteness, beauty, and untapped potential of me. Surrendering to all of that which was internal, was what I held dear to my heart. The sound of my own breath, the beating of my heart, my spirit. These were the things that I knew could never be taken away or damaged. The will to live, regardless of circumstances, kept me tethered as an umbilicus to coexisting in an uncomfortable world. Surrendering to that which I could not control and adapting to destiny brought peace to the war zone that manipulated my mind.

Just as the flower blossom appears as a beautiful creation of nature with its untouched purity, a child comes into life. The plucking of the petals comes from the treatment of others and brings a child to self-sufficiency and inherent doubt. In yoga's child's pose as in life, a person can grow through surrendering to what is, give up control and plant the seeds of tomorrow's growth from today's lessons.

MUSTANG LOTUS
मस्टैंग लोटस

WHAT IS THE ONE THING THAT keeps you here? Nine minutes until midnight and I can't sleep. The yearning of knowing that I am changing is keeping me up. How many times in life do we transform and change who we are? Is this just me who continually peels one layer only to find another layer raw and waiting to be dredged and cleansed from my soul?

It is time to resort to my newfound favorite go-to for centering and peace of mind.

Nasal breathing.

"Oh, dear God, here I am doing the crazy Ayurvedic Indian breathing. I think Yogis that have lived without food for months do this."

Slouched down on my couch with my thumb on one nostril, I exhale and inhale through one side only and then holding the other side, I repeat the intake and feel the cool rush of oxygen in the other nostril. This induces so much clarity of mind and makes my body feel relaxed and alert to the present moment. My breath duplicates the sound of methodical and slowing crashing ocean waves.

Yoga and running work for me but I am always in search of new avenues to discover the depths of who it is that exists within this body. The choice is always our own. We can either choose the light, like the sunshine, or the darkness of a rabbit hole. So, desperately, I seek to find a way up only to be falling again. Tears fall and the heart grasps the emotions tied within the blood and muscles that pump grief, anger, love, sorrow, and pain to every cell that welcomes them.

"Do I even deserve this breath? If it feels so good to take in deep breaths, why does it hurt so much to live? It makes no sense to live a life of regret."

Decades ago, in an elegant light green country club house, I sit drinking a bottle of fancy wine with my friend Antonius from the Netherlands. He says, "If I came up behind you right now and put my hand over your mouth and nose, what would you do?" I respond with, "Grab your hand and pull it off." He exclaims, "If I really did it and would not stop and you could not remove it, what would you do?" I respond with, "Fight like hell." He says, "Exactly, but what would you think about?" With frustration I respond with, "I don't know where you are going with this but I think all I would think about is getting my breath." Antonius remarks, "Yes, and the only separation between life and death is breath. All these things you worry about like money and trivial things disappear when you focus on your breath."

A few more breaths are all I can manage with my runny nose. I choose to be real with myself. I close my eyes and cry out, "God, what is it that is causing this flood of emotion?" Another deep cleansing breath through both nostrils and an exhale with an open mouth and tongue sticking out called "lions' breath" in yogi kingdom. The kid in me loves this so I can imagine sticking my tongue out at the world. Freedom in life is what I dream of and cherish.

When was the last time I felt any freedom? I'm sitting through this damn COVID-19 pandemic and unable to picture the day when I might be able to go on a road trip again. I am just going to close my eyes and imagine my favorite road trip propelling me into a new life.

Over thirty-five Junes ago, throngs of us attending Oregon State University swarm to the Beaver Hut: the local beer joint with dimers night where you get a beer for ten cents. The beer is flowing with plenty of drunk twentysomethings finished with finals. All night study sessions are behind me along with a blue book essay final turned in to pull my grade in Economics from a D to a B. We are ready to unleash for summer!

Elaine says, "Oh my God, there he is!" I ask "Where? I don't see him." She points across the room through the bodies. I am never comfortable in crowds or bars and am always anxious. As the music plays eight-six-seven-five-three-oh-nine, we wait to get checked for ID. She points again and waves. She loudly states in my ear, "Over there, I hope he wants to see me too." The crowd disappears and I gaze across the room to look for him. "Oh yeah, I see him." I wave with a smile. My eyes shift to the left of Rob. I see the face that launches my heart into a crash course with intrigue. We are checked in and weave through a sea of bodies and brown serving trays of shot glass-sized clear plastic cups of beer held over my head. The cocktail waitress hurriedly squawks over the music, "Did you want a tray of dimers?" I mouth to her, "As soon as we get seated." The scent of damp old carpet with spilled beer makes its way up my nose.

The face I see is next to our friend Rob. Elaine charts the way to him as I unknowingly transport across the room and find my way to the group of guys we are here to see. Now, that face that stunned me across the room is staring right at me. The crowded room disappears as my reality becomes single-pointed. He stops me dead in my gasp for air. I am overtaken and sit next to him. He begins the conversation by asking me, "Who are you?" His best friend Rob is a fellow student and acquaintance in a class that I took for an easy A, and he interjects with, "This is Pushpa, she's in my rocks and stars class."

I am enamored. His white smile, round marble green/hazel eyes, long eyelashes and innocent baby face gazes at me. His thick muscular thighs fit into jeans draping over his brown spotless cowboy boots, thus setting the stage for intrigue. My arm reaches over his shoulder, and I ask, "When are you going to ask me out?" *What the hell are you thinking, you idiot! He would never want to go out with you!*

He replies, "How about now?"

My friends who usually get drunk are just getting started for the night as I hold my one beer that slowly inebriates me in my 105-pound body. The room fades and everyone else disappears into the music and darkness of the bar.

And so begins the start of my first mature love relationship. The Norwegian-American engineer wannabe and the lost Indian girl. He is my country boy driving his green rumbling 1968 Ford Mustang with no muffler and listening to Alabama. I am his city girl with my rocker music and concerts to see Journey and hating country music.

That August for my first birthday with my new love, he rolls up and comes to visit me at my apartment. "I wanted to give you something special for your birthday," he says softly. I am terribly embarrassed at getting any gift as he hands me a cassette tape. I look down and laugh.

"Oh, that's great. "It's Alabama and you know how much I love country music."

Scott shyly admits, "I know. I was hoping you might grow to love it as much as I do."

I smile and think to myself, "Uh, okay, but I will never listen to this."

I grow to love it. I think he grows to love me. We are one. Our lives seem to be intertwined as we continue. He spends every night up late and studying. I have met the guy my parents wanted for me. The educated American engineer. Our sentiments are sweet, and our times together are few.

"You are so smart." I speak. His response is always the same. "I just work hard for my grades which are mostly B's. I am not some smart guy." He is also the football player who played defense his freshman and sophomore year for another college on scholarship.

I do not hear his words of insecurity. I only see his perfection of kindness, humility, high intellect, and good looks.

My friends all love telling me how they run into him on campus and how cute he is and how lucky I am. He's the guy that girls find attractive but find him frustrating because he is not flirtatious with them and is very loyal.

Living in a townhome with three other girls has its challenges. Sharon grieves for her mother who died a couple of years ago. Drowning her sorrow in gin and losing her reality in magic mushrooms most nights, Sharon tugs at my heart every morning. With backpack, raingear, and a golf umbrella in hand, I run from my bedroom to wait for Scott to pick me up to walk to class together. I spy Sharon buried in an afghan passed out on the couch in her clothes from the night before like she is every morning. Scott stands at the open door and we both look at her mass of sandy blonde hair and hear the low snores of deep sleep. We glance at each other with a daily familiar feeling of sadness. I say loudly, "Hey Sharon! It's time to go to class." She opens her eyes and rolls over. I yell, "Don't miss class today!" We then walk into the gray drizzly day and slam the door behind us hoping it will awaken her from more than just her sleep.

Another roommate, Kerry, is short and carries her weight in her chest. She sports jeans, tennis shoes, and a sweatshirt every day. Her blonde hair hangs to just above her shoulders. Her boyfriend, Steve, resides with us most of the time. He is the other male that has found his second home with us. They have sex several times per day, and we all hear the pounding on the ceiling. The joke is that we hear the thumping and within a minute, they are done. The other two girls count the number of thumps on the ceiling and predict when it will end. Then there is the other roommate, Sheila, a fiery redhead. She has a 4.0 GPA, has sex with any male that is remotely interested, smokes weed, and drinks beer incessantly. My roommates are each uniquely my friends but two of them seem more lost than myself. That gives me confidence in the choices I am making.

After two years of dating and a romantic summer together in Hawaii, Scott looks towards graduating and starting a career. I am too lost to want to finish school. I am a senior but I just cannot focus and finish. My heart is still not sure that a guy this good could love me.

What does he see in me? It is not like I am a great catch. I have no focus or understanding of who I am or even where I am going. Only that it is with him. The love of my life.

We move in together the summer after he graduates. His parents do not know. We live in a tiny one-bedroom apartment. He works on a road crew for the city, and I am doing odd jobs to pay our bills. I am determined to help him find a better job. Every week, I dial the memorized number to the construction engineering management department at Oregon State and ask if they know anyone who is hiring for a position that Scott would be qualified for. After weeks of calling for him and getting to know the office staff, I finally strike pay dirt. "There is a company looking for a recent grad, but they would need someone in Pittsburgh before coming back to Portland and then maybe to Boston. We are excited about the opportunity and to be able to live in another part of the country for a while. The idea is also easy to accept knowing we will probably come back. He looks to me for guidance as to what to do and my response is to "Go for it. They would be lucky to have you."

In a fury, our fork in the road starts us on a new journey. He accepts the job and within a month we pack a 1970 GMC Truck and pile everything we own in a small U-Haul to begin our cross-country trek. The world seems to lie in the palm of our hands. We are young, have our whole lives ahead of us, and nothing to hold us back. Interstate 80 takes us directly across the United States to Pennsylvania. Two wide-eyed young adults with a recliner, concrete block shelves, a full-sized bed, 13-inch TV, and clothes. Our Don Henley cassette blasts, "I can tell you about my love for you will still be strong after the boys of summer will be gone." Today, the memory evokes the freedom of leaving my past behind me and starting a new life with the man who professes his love for me. It is the journey to exposure, freedom, living life fully, learning new smells, new accents, food, cultures, love, and experiences unimaginable in Oregon.

Breathe in, breathe out. I remember that this is only a memory, but it is so real that every cell in my body relives the beauty of Idaho, views of Salt Lake, the incredible beauty of the rocks of Wyoming, the long straight corn fields of Nebraska, railroads of Chicago, and finally Pittsburgh. The hand that held mine as I sat in the middle of the truck and the loving eyes staring at mine through straightaways create a visceral response.

Why do I have to have such a damn detailed memory? Can I just let this past go?

"I don't understand what happened to our love…" Don Henley sings in my ear. Over 30 years ago and still the music and the memories flood in. "Those days are gone forever. I should just let them go but I can see you…" This makes no sense how my body is nostalgic for a time so long ago and how music can bring me to the point of that moment. There seems no distance between memories and the present. How does love squeeze the distance out of time? Love is timeless and without space.

Thunderstorms roll into Pittsburgh, our new city. Cracking lightning scares the hell out of me as I run screaming from the patio. Inexperienced with storms like this, he laughs as I scream and freak out. I work odd jobs as we both commute to the heart of the city. When we first met, I was his college town girl, and he was my country boy but now we are both getting the 101 on big city living. Neither one of us had experienced the frigid chill of the Three Rivers area of Pittsburgh.

Nine months later, we drive back to Oregon for four months then head to Boston. He works as I move us and organize every detail of our life together. Another new beginning. We have fun with his family and prepare for our upcoming journey to become a married couple.

My parents do not want to do any of the work for the wedding ceremony. Mama D claims, "I am not much for these fancy things but we will do your reception. We can have it on your property by the creek. Down in the trees and by the creek would be so pretty in July." Scott and I are thrilled and sentimental at the idea of it, knowing that one day that property will be ours. She pulls my heart strings at the notion.

Daddy and my brother Jeff build picnic tables and a fire pit for a bonfire. Mama D clears areas within the trees to place tables while keeping the beauty of the natural setting. Some big old oaks with solid wide bases umbrella us for shade. Strong maple trees reach for the sky in praise of our holy union. One old maple that has little stairs built on the side to climb up to reach our tap for maple syrup conjures up images of my small self, climbing up to see if I could reach the maple syrup.

Scott's mother, who has taken me in as her own, asks me to wear her wedding dress. I am honored but do not feel worthy since she has three daughters. "You are the only one of my girls that would fit in it," she states. I reply, "No," to not create waves with my new sisters-in-law but I am so touched that she loves me in this way. I always wanted a mom. She was the kind of mom I wanted. She knew how to have family, how to always love her children, and how to have warmth and love in her home. Her children always came home.

My world seems aligned with love, family, and tons of promise. We get married and head back to the East Coast three months later. We are excited about our new life in Boston. Neither one of us has ever been there but we are excited at the new life we have created together. "Oh my god, I can't believe we are moving to New England. Neither one of us has ever been there!" I say with excitement. Scott responds along with a smile, "Yeah this is exciting to start our lives together, just the two of us."

Two weeks later on a cool, crisp September day, he starts work in the city. He meets me at Logan International with a dozen roses.

He is a flower guy. I love it. We embrace each other and both exude the childlike excitement of our new home. As we leave the airport, we snake through the traffic of a late afternoon rush hour passing and Scott points out the Hari Krishna along our way. He hands me a book from them and says, "I thought you might like this," but I did not know he ever thought about me being from India. I am put off that he would even think of me in the same category. I realize he is just trying to be sweet so I say nothing. I hope I can go back into hiding and he stops seeing me as an Indian woman.

My young man with so much promise becomes the boss and is the project manager of a 31-story high rise at 75 State Street in Boston. For two years, our home is a south shore condo in a suburb. I work in a bank and meet families with direct lineage to the Mayflower. I learn quickly.

History really did happen even though it seems like a story we just heard in school. Plymouth Rock, Boston Tea Party, and the thirteen colonies are not history but the real deal. I'm living it!

Scott ascends quickly among the ranks of leadership and is loved by the people he works with.

I ask most mornings as I lie in bed at 5 a.m., "What time do you think you will be home tonight?" He answers with, "Probably for a late dinner but if you want to come by and have lunch together, we could do that." We plan our occasional lunches and, at times, dinners out.

All I want is to spend time with the love of my life. He is a provider and a conscientious hardworking man, but damn, can we just have some time together?

Our lives have become the fertile ground for a life of transformation and growth. All that we could want is in our palms but all I really want is the guy that can hug me and melt away every feeling of not belonging. He knows how to do it best.

How does one have a full heart and an empty heart at the same time? The fullness based on love transcends forever even after a loved one dies but the emptiness is a product of circumstance. Without a coping skill to handle situations unforeseen, the heart chooses emptiness.

We part after years of loving and have had romantic moments cherished forever. With my heart in my hand, I emerge as a woman hell-bent on leaving and wanting to make my own way. In the darkness of depression and sadness, the time comes and we part.

"Why do we have to part?" I have no answer to his cries. "You weren't there for me when my Indian dad, Thomas, died. I just don't think we need to be together anymore."

He says, "Pushpa, I love you. I would rather have had all those great memories than not. I don't know why it has to end. Don't forget the great quote by Alfred Lord Tennyson, "Tis better to have loved and lost, than never to have loved at all."

I made both of us pay the ultimate price for me having poor judgment in a situation neither one of us had an understanding about: the death of my biological father. At this point, I still had no recollection of his sexual abuse of me.

"BREATHING DEEP IS A WAY to go deeper into the memories." Pamela, the psychotherapist, says. I have been depressed and sad and do not know what to do.

"Keep seeing yourself floating down a river of your life and breathe through every twist and turn of your experience," she continues.

Lying on my back with my eyes closed, I spend the hour with Pamela imagining my river of life. Nothing interesting or emotional comes of it. I pay my one hundred and eighty dollars for the session, jump in my charcoal gray Nissan 300ZX and drive off disappointed. Two blocks away, a left turn somehow stuns me into a black and white film playing in my mind. The car pulls itself over and I break down crying. Sitting for what seems like minutes, the entire memory of Thomas coming towards me with his black hairy mustache and white smile throws me into a tailspin of emotions.

My dad who I was told was a charming, wonderful man was a pedophile. Abused me at his own whim and scarred that part of me that wanted to love the love of my life but could not. My heart was abused too. Taken from me was my ability to truly love. Why the hell do we not talk about the heart of the abused?

With the truth uncovered, our lives redirect to different directions for each of us. Scott marries a woman who tells him she is pregnant on the day that she is having the baby. He calls me crying, "Do you remember the girl, Sally, the girl that I told you I was friends with in Texas? Well, she is in the hospital having my baby, and I don't know what to do." Getting directly to the point, I ask, "Are you in love with her?" Scott is still crying and says, "No."

"It's not like I really want you to marry her, but you have a baby with her now. Are you sure she is telling you the truth? Do you know for sure it is yours? You don't even live in the same state anymore."

"I am pretty sure it is mine, but I don't know."

Once again, he comes to me for advice and like an idiot I proclaim, "Don't do what you did to me when my dad died and leave but, instead, you need to be there for her. You need to marry her."

They marry but three years later, the baby dies.

Downward, I go to places I never imagined. Divorce was never foreseen. There were no red tell-tale signs that this would self-destruct or implode. As an adoptee with no real attachment to my family in India and no interest in ever reconnecting, I had no idea images of my childhood would come between me and the love of my life, causing my heart to break open.

Just as the lotus flower, where every part of the plant is useful, every bit of my history is useful for me to move forward. The lotus can be transformed into so many useful things for human consumption. It can be used for drinking, eating, industrial purposes, or even for packing materials. In the same way, all the pain of my story can be used to survive and help me to flourish into something new. Every pain can be brought from the hellacious place it began to create a beautiful flower that blooms regardless of what conditions in which its roots are planted.

DECADES LATER, I WORK WITH patients with disabilities due to strokes, Parkinson's, and traumatic brain injuries. After Scott, my next marriage, with an alcoholic, comes to an end. I've survived verbal abuse and terror from a man who hates himself and hates women.

After three weeks of crying daily for the loss of the relationship, I realize it was not one of love but just the comfort zone of a man in my life. A new day begins.

This day brought with it a fresh perspective of strength that I could thrive even after the hell of the last ten years.

WORKING AT THE REHABILITATION HOSPITAL in partnership with the YMCA and helping beautiful people who needed a push with their limits becomes a passion of mine. Adaptive wellness is similar to what I am doing with my own personal life. I am broken but it is unseen. My adaptation is internal.

The lotus survives geological changes and still blooms. It was one of the few plants that lived through the Ice Age when many others became extinct.

Working with traumatic brain injury programs has its challenges. The participants can be very impulsive and have behavioral issues. Lots of patience is needed to work with such clients. So far, I had been fortunate. After three months of running this brain injury program, all my participants were sweet and fun.

"Ken, you are doing so well." This participant was elderly and today he had achieved some new milestones with his memory games.

Looking up, I see a six foot three forty-something-year-old man come in and talk with one of the other participants. He is too young to be a stroke patient but presents like it. He grabs my attention. There is a special way about him.

Another participant, Sharon, says, "Hey Bruce, you have to meet Pushpa."

"Nice to meet you, Bruce." A sizzle of energy goes through my body. He is handsome and young looking. Tall and skinny with a big smile. He walks with a cane and his speech is difficult to understand. Regardless, he has a way about him that draws me in and makes me want to know more about him.

He is a survivor of a car accident from 25 years before that left him in a coma for months and then sent him on a different path than originally planned. He was the smart jock who wanted to go to school at Rochester Institute of Technology for biomedical technology, have a family, and a successful career. Instead, he got his bachelor's and master's degrees while in a wheelchair. If only his friend would not have fallen asleep at the wheel, but he did, and he changed the lives of the three others in the car. Killing the young man next to Bruce in the back seat, he left the other two with head injuries. The man now lived three miles away but didn't even have the kindness to be Bruce's friend. Though he ended up as the most successful, he was also the one with the least love in his heart for people with disabilities.

The bastard has five cars and lives a life of entitlement.

Three months later, we end up at the same company party. Bruce is with a date on his arm and I come by myself.

Sharon grabs my arm and pulls me towards Bruce's table. He is sitting with other volunteers at the hospital.

I wait as Sharon grabs him and brings him out to the dance floor. She's a beautiful black woman with a disability and has difficulty with balance and walking. The three of us dance.

Sharon disappears and a slow dance starts. He drops his cane and opens up his arms. We slow dance. A buzzing vibrates in my chest. I ignore it but I feel his warmth and kindness. His date leaves with him.

A week later, the Trans-Siberian Orchestra comes to town and I see a commercial, wishing I could go. A day later, a text comes from Bruce. "Do you want to go to the Trans-Siberian Orchestra with me?"

It's hard to explain how a runner and fitness fanatic ends up in love with a man with a disability. It happens, though, and two years later, we get married.

Five years later, and we are living through a pandemic together. He loves me so much. Two broken people who, together, are unbroken. It is not only me now that lives while surviving a challenging existence. I watch him struggle daily.

Meanwhile, the driver lives an entitled life with no concern for Bruce.

We have our love. We have our mutual desire to stand up for other people and to treat them with goodness.

Lotus flowers are known as living fossils. They are a relic plant since they survived the Ice Age. Though they struggle through the crappy mire they start in, they push through the water to bloom and bring beauty to the world, flowering longer than other flowers. We, too, shall push through this murky mire and find our way to bloom, bringing our own beauty to this world. Thriving after surviving *can* happen. We will survive even the hottest of summers and in difficult spaces anywhere. There is no need to adapt but to use that which becomes a fertile ground for growing to benefit our lives.

So many questions in my life are still unanswered. I have come to understand that my choices have altered every fork in the road of my life. The detriment of those actions live on forever in my mind, but my heart is finally beginning to bloom. By peeling away the layers of entangling roots, my spirit breathes fresh air and I squint while emerging through the murkiness of newfound clarity. Insight reveals the truth: our breath is all we have in creating anew.

About the Author

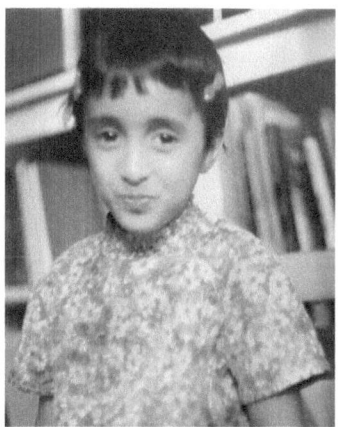 

Pushpa Devi was born into poverty in Calcutta, India and adopted into an American family. She currently lives in Jacksonville, Florida with her husband Bruce and a dog named Belle who barks way too much! She works as a real estate professional and owns a business called Intuitive Life Design. With an uncanny intuitive ability to read where the flow in her clients home or business is stuck, she guides them on how to shift the energy to create change. Pushpa loves playing pickleball every morning and exercise is one of her passions. She enjoys spending time with her family, friends, and traveling as much as possible. She still goes on trips to India and her favorite place to vacation is in Hawaii.